GO!

Starting a

Personal Growth Revolution

Five Steps to Unlock Your Growth & Inspire Growth in Others

Stephen Blandino

GO! Starting a Personal Growth Revolution
Copyright © 2012 by Stephen Blandino

ISBN: 1477627510

ISBN-13: 9781477627518

Library of Congress Control Number: 2012910622

This book is manufactured in the United States.

Cover design by Josh Childs
Editing by Brannon Golden and Trisha Heddlesten

——— *Starting a* ———
Personal Growth Revolution
Five Steps to Unlock Your Growth & Inspire Growth in Others

Stephen Blandino

To Karen and Ashley

You are the two most important people in the world to me.
I couldn't ask for a more wonderful family.
I love you deeply and love sharing life
with both of you.

Praise for *GO! Starting a Personal Growth Revolution*

"Some books are written to inform, and others to inspire, still others to motivate you to action. In *GO! Starting a Personal Growth Revolution* author Stephen Blandino does all three. You will learn, grow and move forward. The concepts are real-life and the strategies, if followed, will actualize your full capacity potential."

– DR. SAMUEL R. CHAND

Leadership Coach, Consultant, and Author of
Cracking Your Church's Culture Code
(www.samchand.com)

"Anybody who wants to become all that God wants them to be has to read *GO!* Stephen hits the nail on the head on how we develop personally so that we can maximize our God given potential!"

– HERBERT COOPER

Lead Pastor, People's Church, Oklahoma City

"In business I'm always looking for a competitive edge, and in *GO! Starting a Personal Growth Revolution* Stephen Blandino gives you that edge. Through the five levels of personal growth you create a pathway for personal growth both for yourself and the people you lead. This book is one you'll actually implement the wisdom it contains."

– BILL BARNETT

Nationally Syndicated Radio Host and Best Selling Author of
Are You DUMB Enough to be RICH?

"Stephen takes the mystery out of personal growth. He shows me how to be intentional about growth in my own life, and also how I can help others (my family, friends, mentees, so on) develop as well. *GO! Starting a Personal Growth Revolution* is full of the most practical wisdom you'll find anywhere."

– JEFF GALLEY

Team Leader for LifeGroups & Missions, LifeChurch.tv

"The best growth plan is the one that works for you. I know the GO Practices you will discover in *GO! Starting a Personal Growth Revolution* work because I have watched Stephen Blandino practice them for years. Create your personalized Growth TRAC and get moving to the next level today. Then take someone with you tomorrow!"

– STEVE MOORE

President, Missio Nexus, and Author of
***Who Is My Neighbor? Being a Good Samaritan
in a Connected World***

"Stephen is onto a much needed step-by-step approach to personal growth. Packed with stories, *GO!* is a great read embedded with a number of life-changing practices. I came away with several practical next steps and I'm sure you will too!"

– MARK HOWELL

Small Group Ministry Consultant and Coach

"I have had the privilege to know and work with Stephen Blandlino for over 25 years. One constant during these years has been Stephen's commitment to personal growth. His personal journey has now been encapsulated into this outstanding work to help each of us overcome our growth gaps. This is a must read!"

– DARIUS JOHNSTON

Lead Pastor, Christ Church, Fort Worth, Texas

"If personal growth and development seems mysterious to you, or if achieving sustained meaningful growth has eluded you, this book has the keys that can help you unlock your true growth potential! Five clear and powerful steps will put you on TRAC to live the life you have always wanted to live, realize your full potential and help others reach their full potential. Start your Growth Revolution today!"

– JERRY HURLEY

Team Development Leader, LifeChurch.tv

"God did not give you the potential to pursue great dreams only to see those dreams die in the desert". With this work, Blandino presents a thoughtful, compelling and life-giving approach to personal growth that is both serious and inspirational. With the array of information provided the author has succeeded in constructing an extremely valuable and inspirational resource for all seeking to grow to their full capacity and helping others do the same. It will encourage and empower us to listen for and embody our innate callings in God."

– DR. DORIS GOMEZ
Assistant Professor & Program Director,
M.A. in Organizational Leadership,
Regent University School of Global Leadership & Entrepreneurship

"Stephen Blandino's latest book gets right to the heart of personal growth. *GO! Starting a Personal Growth Revolution* shares the stories of ordinary people doing extraordinary things, shows you how to unlock that power in your life, and gives you the strategies to overcome the obstacles that lie in your way. This book will challenge you, as it has me, to strive for more and to maximize potential. Read it and be inspired to go the extra mile, guaranteed."

– DR. CALVIN H. LAWRENCE
Tarleton State University

Contents

Introduction

The human heart—*your* heart—is alive with enormous God-given potential. Your potential—that tightly wound ball of latent possibilities—is rumbling like an earthquake below the ocean floor ready to unleash the tsunami of your dreams. Perhaps you're one of the lucky few whose dreams are consuming the shores of your world. Or maybe you're like the masses, frustrated by the glaring gap that exists between your dreams and your current circumstances.

The gap, although filled with potential, feels like a barren desert. Feelings of frustration, disappointment, and even paralysis thrive in the gap where aspirations gasp to stay alive. Hope dwindles in the gap. Life becomes mind-numbingly routine. The path to your dreams seems to be buried under miles of sand dunes. In the desolate gap, our biggest fear is that our dreams will drift slowly away like a mirage, and that our lives will not matter. But it doesn't have to be that way.

God did not give you the potential to pursue great dreams only to see those dreams die in the desert. He called you to close the gap between *what if* and *what is* by growing to your full capacity and helping others do the same. And that process happens best by climbing the five levels of personal growth.

The Five Levels of Personal Growth

I can still remember sitting in my office, wrestling with some crucial decisions. Life was good and my professional career was going well. The people I served were growing, leaders were developing, and I was making progress toward my goals. Thinking about the decisions before me, it suddenly dawned on me—what I *did* was impacting what I *do*. The steps I took yesterday were affecting the decisions I had to make today. Let me explain.

Several months prior, I attended a lunch featuring a respected leadership speaker and author. After enjoying a meal with other leaders at my table, the featured speaker took the stage. For no more than 30 minutes, he shared several important principles from his latest book. His experience, credibility, and proven leadership gave him the authority to share his leadership ideas. And his down-to-earth communication style connected well with his audience. One idea he shared jumped out at me with such intensity that it literally *changed my life!* This leadership author challenged every person in the room to develop a personal growth plan—not just for a year, but every year for the rest of our lives.

Before this encounter, I had taken a few steps to develop my potential, but I had never created a written personal growth plan. My growth was more like a pinball machine, bouncing around sporadically with no rhyme or reason. As I listened to the challenge, I knew I needed help.

I immediately purchased two leadership curriculums to serve as a road map for my growth. These courses, complete with audio teachings, videos, and workbooks, were the core of my first growth plan. I decided to come into the office an hour early each day, listen to a leadership resource, reflect on what I was learning, and figure out how I could apply it to my life. My growth plan wasn't rocket science, but it gave me some desperately needed direction. Week after week I followed my plan, and slowly, I began to notice a shift—*the more I learned the more my thinking changed.*

As I sat in my office one morning, processing a series of leadership decisions, it suddenly dawned on me—what I *did* months ago was positively impacting the decisions I was making that day. In fact, what I had learned was not only shaping my thinking, but was determining the actions that would follow. Those actions would impact the people I lead. And the people I impacted would ultimately influence others.

That morning, in a matter of moments, the power of personal growth became clear to me. I recognized the transformation that had occurred in me, and its ability to influence those around me and beyond me. I quickly pulled out a piece of paper and wrote down *Learning, Thinking, Living, Impacting,* and *Multiplying*—the five levels of personal growth.

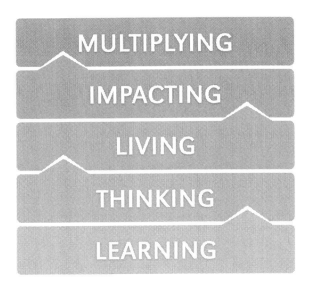

Like a chemical reaction in a laboratory, stimulated by a catalyst, your personal growth is the catalyst that puts your dreams in reach. However, personal growth was never meant to stop with you. As you climb the five levels, you ignite a revolution—a *personal growth revolution*—in you *and* around you. At the highest level of growth, your revolution moves from an internal force to an external movement.

My discovery of the five levels of personal growth began in 1998. Since that time, my understanding of each level has grown exponentially, and I've watched the remarkable difference they've made in my life and others. Like throwing a rock into a pond and watching the ripples form one after another, I have witnessed the far-reaching effects of personal growth. My hope for you is that by engaging in this process, you too will experience and inspire a growth revolution.

A Personal Growth Pathway
and a People-Development Process

Each of the five levels of personal growth is a step toward initiating personal development, transforming thinking, altering behavior, and influencing others. In fact, they are both a *pathway* and a *process*. **The five levels are a *pathway to personal growth* and a *process to develop people*.** The first three levels are inward focused and provide a pathway to personal development. The last two levels are outward focused and provide a process to people development. In the following pages, I'll unpack the *characteristics* of each level as well as the *practice* that puts each level in reach.

So what happens if you are not naturally inclined to grow? **What if your personal growth needs a jumpstart before**

you can ascend the five levels? While all of us face ups and downs in the personal growth journey, the reality is that many people spend an entire lifetime with their personal growth button on pause. Their growth gap is like a permanent fixture in the landscape of their dreams. They need some kind of encounter, experience, or shift in attitude that will push their "play button" for future growth. So before we discuss the five levels of personal growth and how you can experience and inspire a personal growth revolution, I want to address two growth realities: *gaps* and *on-ramps*. This is where our personal growth journey begins, so enjoy!

PART ONE

Gaps and On-Ramps

—————— *Chapter 1* ——————

Gaps

Growing up, all Jennifer ever wanted was to be a wife and stay-at-home mom. Her earliest memories of being five years old, rocking her baby sister in a rocking chair and imagining when she would one day have her own baby, stayed with her into adulthood. While her high school friends were choosing colleges because of their great pre-med programs and strong business schools, Jennifer looked for a school with a great elementary education program. Why? It wasn't because she wanted to teach. Jennifer chose to get her teacher certification because if she ever HAD to work, at least she could keep the same schedule as her kids.

Jennifer eventually had three children, and loved staying home with them during their early years. For more than ten years she spent everyday caring for her home, taking her children on adventures, and being a companion to her husband. But something in Jennifer changed as the kids grew older and developed more independence. Jennifer said she "had no life outside of them," and no idea what to do with herself now that they didn't need her constant attention.

Her growing uneasiness was compounded when she attended a class I was teaching on the subject of life purpose. I prodded Jennifer with questions about her dreams, desires, and purpose, and what she was doing to develop them. Her curiosity was so engaged that she took the class twice. Jennifer said, "What I learned was perhaps the scariest idea that has ever occurred to me. I had NO idea what I wanted, where I was headed, or what I even liked. I had been so devoted to the growth of my family that I had completely neglected my own."

The Year of Jennifer

Jennifer told me that her personal growth road map was so entirely blank that she felt desperate measures were in order. So she sat down with her husband and children, looked them in the eyes with bold resolve, and declared, "This is The Year of Jennifer!" Jennifer carefully explained that she was going to put herself first for one year and focus on developing herself personally. She was going to cook what she liked, watch and read whatever interested her, make spontaneous trips to get coffee or meet a friend, and take time to learn what her passions were. Jennifer wanted to discover her God-given potential and how to use her strengths beyond being a wife and mother. Though being a devoted wife and mother was one of her callings, it was not her *only* calling.

Jennifer admitted that for the first few months she felt extremely guilty and selfish. She had spent years putting everyone else first, and caring for her own needs and wants didn't come easily. Declaring "The Year of Jennifer" might sound like the height of self-centered egotism, but Jennifer is truly a selfless person. She has a deeply compassionate spirit. She cares about her friends and expresses genuine love for her family.

Several times Jennifer came close to calling it quits, but she couldn't shake the nagging questions in the back of her mind about her future. Derek, her husband, provided constant encouragement and accountability to keep her from abandoning her mission. And when my wife Karen and I spent time with Derek and Jennifer over dinner, the conversation inevitably turned to personal growth.

As the "Year of Jennifer" progressed, Jennifer caught glimpses of who she could become. To keep focused, she created a poster filled with magazine clippings that represented the life she wanted. She chose words, phrases, and pictures that had an emotional attraction to her and hung the poster in a spot where she would see it daily. She surrounded herself with books about finding personal strengths, callings, destiny, and "sweet spots."

In daily living situations she often asked herself, "Does this take me closer to where I want my life to be or further from it?" And if Jennifer couldn't answer, she recalled the images on her poster to remind her of where she was headed. Although it seemed elementary at times, it worked powerfully in her life.

As the year drew to a close, Jennifer actually felt a little sad that the "Year of Jennifer" was ending. She recalled, "What had started as an exercise in guilt actually ended in a wonderful new relationship...with myself. For the first time in my adult life I knew what I liked, what I wanted, and the beginnings of where I wanted my life to go. Above all, I realized that there shouldn't be any sadness about my year coming to an end. I have before me the 'Life of Jennifer' and it is mine for the taking." Her revolution was just beginning.

Maybe you can relate to how Jennifer felt. Perhaps you're staring at your own "blank personal growth slate" wondering what on earth your life is becoming. Maybe years have flown by and the only thing that's changed is the number of wrinkles on your forehead, the number of emotional scars in your soul, or the number of times a movie of dashed dreams has played over and over in your mind. Like Jennifer, you might be scratching your head in bewilderment as your eyes lock on the gap that exists between where you are now and where you ultimately want to be.

Facing Your Gap

All of us have gaps. My friend Steve Moore refers to these gaps as our *"capacity challenge"*.[1] The capacity challenge is the gap between the person you are *today* and the person you must *become* to reach your dreams. The following diagram best illustrates your ultimate God-given capacity, how much of your potential is being reached, and the remaining gap between the two.

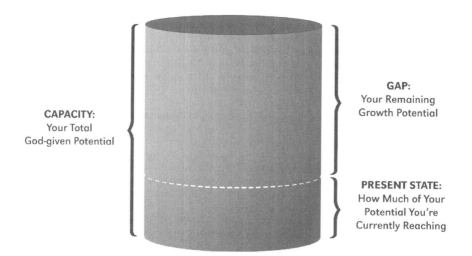

GAP:
Your Remaining
Growth Potential

CAPACITY:
Your Total
God-given Potential

PRESENT STATE:
How Much of Your
Potential You're
Currently Reaching

Capacity defines *what a person can contain.* It is the total of your God-given potential. In the same way a milk carton has the capacity to hold a gallon of milk, God created every one of us with a specific capacity. In some areas of life, your capacity is like a gallon, in others it's like a quart, and in still others it's like a pint. Put simply, your strengths are greater in some areas than others. The more you understand your *greatest strengths* (how God uniquely designed you), the more you will understand where you have the largest capacity for personal growth. Let me give you some personal examples.

My capacity for leadership is greater than my capacity for basketball. My capacity for teaching is far greater than my capacity for music. My capacity for writing exceeds my capacity for counseling. No matter how hard I work to grow the low-capacity areas of my life, my performance in these areas will only marginally improve. In areas of weakness, I am limited by a very low capacity ceiling. It's not a matter of effort or desire. It's completely a matter of capacity.

> *The gifts and passions God builds in to you define the areas where you have the greatest capacity and aptitude for growth.*

If I acquired leadership coaching, my leadership abilities could grow by say, 20 percent. However, no matter how many basketball camps I diligently participate in, I will *never* excel on the basketball court. Simply stated, my capacity for growth in leadership, teaching, and writing will always outperform my capacity for basketball, music, and counseling. The same is true for you: The gifts and passions God builds in to you define the areas where you have the greatest capacity and aptitude for growth.

Your Present State

Your growth gap is like the half-full cup in the diagram above. The size of your gap is felt the most when you understand your *present state*...that is, how much of your potential you're currently reaching. The cup might have the *capacity* to hold twelve ounces, but your present state may show you reaching only 40 percent of your potential. This is a crucial point to understand: just because your life *has* capacity for growth doesn't mean it *will automatically* be filled to capacity.

Many people go through life with the capacity to do far more than they're currently even trying. They're only realizing half of their potential because they haven't developed the other half. Only by developing ALL of our potential can we reach our full God-given capacity and, ultimately, fulfill the mission He created us for. When you grow consistently, you're closing the gap between being half-full and being filled to the brim.

This gap is what Jennifer came face-to-face with and resolved to do something about. She had to acknowledge her present state, capture a dream for her life, look squarely at the gap between the two, and then take action to close that gap. And that's exactly what she did. One year after the "Year of Jennifer" came to an end, Jennifer completed her first full-time semester of grad school. Her satisfaction level, sense of purpose, and understanding of God's plan for her life is clearer than ever. Jennifer's personal growth revolution has begun.

The gap is a reality in all of our lives. Nobody is immune to the gap, but how people respond to it is as diverse as the gap itself. Some people don't even recognize that a gap exists. They struggle with nearsightedness, walking obliviously past every opportunity to grow. Others acknowledge the gap in some areas of their life but ignore it in others. They grow cafeteria style, thinking, "I'll take a little bit of this and a little bit of that." Still, others take their growth gaps seriously, choosing to grow on purpose in strategic areas of their life.

Think about the faces of the growth gap in your own world. Why can some of your business friends grow thriving companies...and others can't? How come some of your kids' teachers create powerful learning moments in their classrooms while others do nothing more than count the minutes until the next bell rings? Why do some pastors break growth barriers while others remain trapped under a lid? Believe it or not, it's not about desire—it's all about *reaching God-given capacity.* The individuals who consistently achieve superior outcomes choose to close the gap between who they are and who they must become. In other words, they face their personal growth gaps head-on and pay the price to close them.

Your "Be/Do" Capacity

What did God create *you* with the capacity to *be* and *do*? The "be" part of that question is all about your character. It focuses on your spiritual, relational, emotional, and physical health. The "do" part of that question is all about your contribution. It focuses on the difference you will make in your world through your gifts, abilities, skills, and passions. The "be" and the "do" both require personal growth because your life has gaps in both areas.

Your "be" capacity is quite large. God believes in who you can be because His Spirit has the power to form His character within you. Your willingness to cooperate with His work is a huge part of this process. And your commitment to grow in the right disciplines—spiritually, relationally, emotionally, and physically—will turn you into a person you've only dreamed of becoming.

Your "do" capacity is also larger than you think. Consider this: if God created you with the capacity (the basic gifts, abilities, skills, and passions) to lead a multi-million dollar company, and that's the dream He's put in your heart, then you can fully realize that dream *if* you grow your potential to its full capacity. If God created you with the capacity to serve the poor, and He's birthed a dream inside of you to make a dent in poverty, then you should grow your potential for serving to its full capacity. And if God made you with the capacity to teach

> *Dreams minus growth equals illusion. Capacity minus growth equals regret.*

kindergarten students, and your heart exudes joy when you're investing in the next generation, then you should grow your potential for loving and teaching kids to its full capacity. Dreams minus growth equals illusion. Capacity minus growth equals regret.

Author and cultural architect Erwin McManus captures the "do" part of your capacity best when he asks, "Is your dream worth your life?" Is what you imagine enough to drive you, to propel you, to motivate you to grow in whatever way necessary to achieve it? If your dream is rummaging through the basement of your capacity, then you're not dreaming big enough. Let the Holy Spirit awaken you to the mission God is carrying out in the world. In His mission you will discover a glorious dream worth pursuing. That's what Jennifer did. And that's what you can do, too.

Discovering Your "Be/Do" Capacity

Jesus was the ultimate example of what it meant to "be." Yes, He was God, an obvious advantage over you and me. But He was also a man. He was tempted, challenged, ridiculed, cursed, and crucified. He had every opportunity to "be" anything but pure, loving, compassionate, focused, and disciplined. So if you want to discover your "be" capacity, read Scriptures about who God has called you to be. Passages like the "Sermon on the Mount" (Matthew 5-7), the "Great Commandment" (Matthew 22:34-40) and the "Fruit of the Spirit" (Galatians 5:22-23) are just the tip of the iceberg when it comes to our capacity for "being." God wouldn't have called us to "be" like this if it were not possible. The key to remember is that it is only possible with the help of the Holy Spirit.

"Doing" is the other side of the capacity coin. Ephesians 2:10 says, "We are God's workmanship, created in Christ Jesus to do good works, which God prepared in advance for us to do." Several years ago, I finally got serious about discovering the "do" part of my capacity. I started by answering some of life's big questions (similar to many of the questions Jennifer asked herself). These questions helped me understand where I had the greatest "do" capacity for growth and, ultimately, the greatest capacity to make a difference. Try this exercise. Ask yourself these questions:

> *Where have I experienced the most success?*
> *What are my greatest strengths, abilities, and skills?*
> *What do I have the deepest passion for?*
> *What kind of personality do I have?*
> *Where do I receive the greatest return on my investment of time?*

You'll find that each question is linked to your largest capacity containers for "doing"—your gifts, abilities, passions, and personality. Once you've answered these capacity-revealing questions, look for the common threads woven among your answers. Your most common responses will reveal two things: how God has wired you to make your greatest contribution to the world, and where you have the greatest capacity for personal growth. Those are important insights. When I took the time to answer these questions for myself, I discovered my purpose in life and the areas in which I needed to grow in order to see that purpose fully realized.

Don't be a stranger to yourself. Get the first glimpses of your capacity. Envision who you want to "be" and what you want to "do." Discovering your "be/do" capacity will help you better understand your specific growth gaps.

Just How Big is My Capacity?

That's a question I don't believe any of us can truly answer. Discovering your "be/do" capacity with the exercises above is an important first step. However, even after taking that step, the humbling truth is that we often don't realize our God-given capacity until we start aggressively pursuing the five levels of personal growth. Today's growth usually reveals tomorrow's potential. And tomorrow's potential gives us one more glimpse of our ultimate capacity. Craig Groeschel, Senior Pastor of LifeChurch.tv, says that one key to creating personal spiritual momentum is to "do today what I can do, to enable me to do tomorrow what I can't do today."[2] That same principle applies to every area of your life.

> Today's growth usually reveals tomorrow's potential. And tomorrow's potential gives us one more glimpse of our ultimate capacity.

My wife discovered this principle in her own life. After high school, Karen graduated with a two-year college degree and then immediately moved into full-time employment. After serving in a variety of jobs for several years, she went to work for a major airline. As a part of her orientation, she had to complete six weeks of intensive training. To her surprise, she aced the training. Karen later told me that her success in those training sessions gave her the confidence to go back to school and finish her four-year degree. Until then, she couldn't see herself in college again.

Yesterday's growth helped Karen see tomorrow's potential. And tomorrow's potential gave her glimpses of her capacity. And on the day she graduated with a Bachelor's degree, something rose up inside of her as she watched Master's students cross the stage to receive their diplomas. In her heart she said, "One day that will be me." And one day it was. At the end of 2009, Karen graduated with a Master's and is now serving full-time as a counselor in a public elementary school. When you grow on purpose, what seemed impossible yesterday looks possible today.

The "gap" is why you're not already reaching your full "be/do" capacity. You don't have the ability to be and do today what you will have the capacity to be and do tomorrow. That almost sounds like a contradiction, so let me say it another way—you have not developed your character, gifts, skills, abilities, and knowledge in such a way that God can entrust you with greater responsibility today. God has already given you the capacity to handle greater opportunities. Now He's waiting on you to significantly invest in your personal growth. When you do, your potential will mature and He'll be able to trust you with increased opportunities aligned with His purpose for your life.

Refocus and Don't Quit

Capacity is the *container size of your life* as determined by God. **Nothing you can do will change the size of the container—only how full the container becomes.** You may not have control over your capacity, but you have complete control over your potential. And even though you don't know what your full capacity is, I would suggest it's much, much larger than you think.

If you are intentional every day to learn and grow, you'll be utterly amazed at what you can accomplish over a lifetime. Choose to be personally and Biblically true to who God created you to be and what God created you to do. And don't compare yourself with someone else's capacity—only measure yourself by your own capacity. That's where your greatest opportunity for growth is.

As glimpses of your "be/do" capacity become clear, you'll quickly feel the pain of your growth gaps. In fact, when you look at the size of your growth gaps, you might even see a striking resemblance to the Grand Canyon. Like Jennifer, you'll probably want to quit. But don't. Instead, refocus. Acknowledge your gaps. They are your current reality, but they don't have to be your permanent reality. Maybe it's time for your own "Year of You"—not from a selfish perspective, of course, but from a growth-focused perspective. Set your sights on your God-given dreams and capacity, and then look for the on-ramps to personal growth. The on-ramps are where growth revolutions begin. That's where we turn our attention next.

--------- *Chapter 2* ---------

On-Ramps

'm not the best driver in the world. I'm not even the best driver in my house. Karen reminds me at least once a week of the "gap" that exists in my driving skills. I'm convinced she's still harboring bad feelings from our courtship—when I picked her up in my '76 AMC Hornet, a car my dad picked up as "a sweet deal" at one of those government auctions. Affectionately dubbed the Smurfmobile by my friends, it was an obscenely, blindingly bright blue. Adding insult to injury, the plate on the dashboard that was supposed to say "Hornet" was missing the "t." Only a guy would actually drive a "Horn-e." Needless to say, any time Karen and I went out on a date, we drove her sporty red Honda CRX. Even though it looked like a tennis shoe on wheels, her CRX put the "Horn-e" to shame any day of the week.

My friends and co-workers also frequently remind me of my driving inadequacies. Ben called one rainy afternoon to ask me to pick him up because he and his broken bike were stranded. Just a few minutes after I picked him up in a torrential down-pour, Ben—clutching the dashboard—said simply, "Stephen, you're scaring me." I tried to laugh it off, saying, "I'm scaring myself."

The truth is, I get impatient in stop-and-go traffic, so I tend to take it as a personal challenge to rev up and close the gap between me and the car ahead as fast as I can. I prefer to stop the same way, pacing myself to hit the brakes at the last possible moment...even when it's raining.

For someone like me who hates stoplights and stop signs, the highway is another story. As long as it's not rush hour, I'd just as soon take an on-ramp to a nearby interstate. Although my driving isn't any better on the highway—one time I ran the "Horn-e" into the back of my wife's mobile tennis shoe on I-20—at least I can efficiently get where I want to go. On-ramps are my friends. They're like the entry points to accelerated progress. Personal growth has on-ramps too.

Accessing the Five Levels of Personal Growth

The on-ramps in your life give you rapid access to the five levels of personal growth. To experience a growth revolution for yourself, you have to get out of the stop-and-go traffic of your normal, growth-resistant routines. You have to access the on-ramps. On-ramps are the growth attitudes that make lifelong learning possible. On-ramps aren't the five levels of personal growth; they're simply the wide-open access points where you get on. They give you the right mindset to *enter* the five levels where you'll close your growth gaps and help others do the same.

> *On-ramps are the growth attitudes that make lifelong learning possible.*

For many people, their growth on-ramps are dependent on another person. In other words, they take their cues for growth from a spouse, a close friend, an employer, a teacher, a professor, or their church. They rely on clear suggestions or advice, assignments, classes, or even a formal syllabus. Unfortunately, if that sounds like you, your on-ramps will close the moment that person steps out of your life. You lose your way and your will for personal growth, and your gaps become a permanent fixture in the landscape of your life. Your on-ramps—the attitudes that propel you toward growth—are ultimately your own responsibility. If you're willing to grow, you have to learn where to go.

The Three On-Ramps

Positive growth attitudes are the on-ramps to the five levels of personal growth. They route you around the traffic jams of mediocrity, taking you directly onto the fast track toward a personal growth revolution. The three on-ramp attitudes are humility, curiosity, and resilience.

HUMILITY

Several years ago, I assumed a new leadership position that required a steep learning curve. Although I was going to be doing things I had never done before, I was confident that I possessed the skill set I would need to be successful. The easy road would have been for me to try to "fake it till you make it," but I knew that wasn't a good long-term strategy.

Shortly after taking the role, I happened to meet a man who was considered to be one of the foremost experts in our field. He was launching a one-year training center in our city and I knew I wanted—actually, needed—to be a part of it. There was only one problem: investing in it would cost $10,000.

In a meeting with the finance committee, I presented this as a once-in-a-lifetime opportunity. I can still remember one member saying, "Stephen, you already have the skills to pull this off. Why do you need to join this training center?" In that moment I had a decision to make: I could accept the affirmation of this committee member and allow my ego to trump the growth opportunity, or I could humble myself and admit that I also needed the training myself. I chose what was behind door number two. The finance committee decided that if I could find the money in my budget, I could do it. That $10,000 represented more than one-third of my department's budget for the entire year, but I had to accept the risk.

Was it worth it? Less than six months after completing the training, that ministry doubled in size. Humility feels emotionally expensive, but pride costs you much more—in the growth potential that it steals.

All personal growth requires humility. Without humility, pride takes the wheel and aims for the ditch. History is littered with the pages of brilliant and talented men and women who were ultimately destroyed by their own pride.

Humility reveals our humanity. Let that idea really take hold in your mind. Humility reveals your humanity by keeping your failures and your successes in proper perspective to each other. Humility makes you teachable, a constant reminder of how much you need lifelong learning.

Abraham Lincoln, an avid reader and voracious learner, understood the importance of humility. When some editors were preparing a directory of congressmen, they asked Lincoln to submit his biography. He humbly wrote, "Education defective." He was keenly aware that even though he had closed many of his personal growth gaps, humility was still the key to all future learning.

When we lack humility, our pride builds our knowledge into monuments of our own greatness. Although we can't see it at the time, those monuments are actually barriers and roadblocks to our future learning. Humility, on the other hand, is like the gatekeeper to growth—and its gates are always open. If we begin to value what we've already learned over what we have yet to learn, those gates slam shut, sealed tight with the padlock of pride. Your current knowledge cannot be the permanent watermark for your future. Past learning does not guarantee future growth.

Your current knowledge cannot be the permanent watermark for your future. Past learning does not guarantee future growth.

In the Beatitudes, Jesus was crystal clear about the importance of humility. Matthew 5 begins, "Blessed are the poor in spirit, for theirs is the kingdom of heaven."[3] Professor and author Bruce Winston observes, "'Poor in spirit' is a state of being opposite of 'rich in pride.'"[4] Winston says that we should not view ourselves as a full cup—something that cannot receive more— but rather as an empty cup, always willing to learn more from others. Humility reminds us just how empty our cup really is. Humility helps us remember that what filled our cup yesterday won't continue to fill our cup today.

Humility calls us to increasingly depend on God, acknowledging that His infinite wisdom far surpasses our finite minds. Proverbs 1:7 captures it best: "Start with God—the first step in learning is bowing down to God; only fools thumb their noses at such wisdom and learning" (MSG). Bowing implies submission, respect, honor, reverence, and humility. Without this lifelong learning posture of the heart, we'll enthrone our knowledge as an idol and turn God into our footstool. Humble yourself! Doing so will give you the attitude you need to access the five levels of personal growth and ultimately close your growth gaps. Is your posture bent toward humility? Or are you drowning in the glory of your own press release?

What's the easiest way to cultivate humility? It's simple: shut up! Seriously. We all like to talk about ourselves. The problem is, so does the person we're talking to. When you put a verbal zip tie on your mouth, it might surprise you how much more people will enjoy hanging out with you.

CURIOSITY

Curiosity is the second on-ramp to personal growth. Have you ever noticed how inquisitive toddlers are? They constantly investigate their surroundings, always looking for something new. Their curiosity is like a wind in their sails, tugging on their minds to explore. Unfortunately, the older we get, the more that wind dies down, replaced with the stillness of apathy.

Apathy is a perfectly natural response that settles in once we've learned enough to survive. This principle applies equally to our personal and professional lives. When you lose your curiosity at work, it's because you've learned enough to keep your job. When you lose your curiosity at home, it's because you've learned enough to stay married. When you lose your curiosity spiritually, it's because you've grown content in your relationship with God. Replacing curiosity with apathy is the first step toward losing the comfort we've fought so hard to maintain. Eventually the world we've become comfortable with is going to be disrupted yet again:

"We're going to have to let you go."

"I think I want a divorce."

Or worst of all: "Depart from me, I never knew you."[5]

Of the three on-ramps, curiosity is the one that's most proactive. It's like a built-in thruster that skyrockets your growth to entirely new levels.

The great inventor Thomas Edison possessed an unquenchable curiosity for learning. He was known as the "Wizard of Menlo Park," named after his laboratory in New Jersey, where he brought to life such inventions as the light bulb and the phonograph. As his work continued to expand, he constructed the largest testing laboratory in the world in West Orange, New Jersey. There's a story that a new staff member asked him about the company's rules. Edison gruffly answered, "There ain't no rules around here. We're trying to accomplish something." And accomplish he did. Before his death at the age of 84, Edison was credited with 1,093 patents. His curiosity never slept.

RESILIENCE

Often overlooked, resilience is your third on-ramp to personal growth. It's also perhaps the most distinctive of the on-ramps. Resilience is your ability to adjust, to recover easily from stress, negative circumstances, or change. While curiosity is proactive, resilience is responsive. Resilience is all about how well you choose to respond to the trials and circumstances that life throws at you.

How you respond during difficult times will determine whether you leverage those challenges to help you learn and grow—or allow them to derail your life. The resilience on-ramp is God's life shaping process. It's the school of hard knocks that God uses to mold our character. Now, that doesn't mean God sponsors every class—if He did, that would mean He is the cause of all of our pain and suffering. The truth is, most of these life-shaping classes are sponsored by our own poor decisions, pain brought on by others, or circumstances beyond our control. The source of the pain doesn't necessarily matter; our response to it does. If we can be resilient and positive, we can bounce back and ultimately pass the test.

> The resilience on-ramp is God's life shaping process.

Lisa Beamer discovered firsthand the difficulty of the life shaping process. On September 11, 2001, her husband Todd, a software salesman for Oracle, boarded United Airlines flight 93. He had just returned from a family vacation in Europe. Rather than taking the original flight he had set up for September 10, he rescheduled so he could spend one more night with his wife and children before heading back to work. The horrific terrorist events of 9/11 changed everything.

Life had thrown Lisa and her children the ultimate curve ball—making her a widow and her kids fatherless. Lisa could have allowed bitterness, anger, and rage to set in and overwhelm her with despair. But she chose to be resilient.

In an NBC Dateline interview less than one year later, Stone Phillips asked Lisa a sobering question: "Can you ever forgive the hijackers?" Her response revealed her deep faith. She began by explaining how counterproductive bitterness and anger can be. Then she said, "I won't allow someone else's terrible actions to turn me into a person that I don't want to be."[6]

Lisa Beamer could have easily become jaded. Instead, like clay in the hands of a potter, Lisa allowed God to restore her heart. And through her pain she developed a depth of character greater than many of us will ever know. Did God cause Lisa and her family's pain? Absolutely not! But Lisa wasn't willing to waste that pain—she grew because of how she responded to it.

This shaping journey will look different for every person. For some it will include people, pain—and sometimes people who are a pain—temptation, or uncontrollable events. For others it will involve a series of integrity checks and obedience checks. While God certainly isn't the author of all of our pain, He *does* want to bring good out of the pain. The apostle Paul offered some great perspective: "And we know that in all things God works for the good of those who love him, who have been called according to his purpose."[7]

As much as you hate it, pain is a critical ingredient for growth. Your character grows the most during the difficult seasons of life—it's rarely stretched when things are going great. And your response is the common denominator in the good times and the hard times. It can spark growth or kill it. As former NFL coach Lou Holtz said, "Life is ten percent what happens to you and ninety percent how you respond to it."

So how have you responded to life lately? If "10" equals "My response couldn't have been better" and "1" equals "My response set off an emotional or relational World War III," how would you rate yourself? You can't change your response if you can't admit where you are currently. So what's your score? And what would it take to bump your score up two points?

Each of the on-ramps—humility, curiosity, and resilience—bolster your ascent up the five levels of personal growth. They make growth revolutions possible for yourself and the people you influence. At the same time, while each on-ramp initiates personal growth, there's an equal and opposite exit-ramp that can kill it. Pride can displace humility. Apathy can overtake curiosity. And the difficulties of life shaping can shift our focus from resilience to hard-heartedness. Furthermore, each on-ramp is necessary to sustain your forward progress up the five levels of personal growth. If you don't get anything else, you need to get this: **It might only take one growth attitude to lead you onto the five levels of personal growth, but it takes all of them to keep you there.** You cannot continue to ascend each level without humility to keep you teachable, curiosity to keep you learning, and resilience to keep you moving.

What's Next

Are you ready to enter the five levels of personal growth? Are you ready to close your growth gaps? Do you crave a life that's transformed by personal growth and inspires others' growth? You have to match your yearning for growth with an unwavering commitment to the on-ramps. Humility, curiosity, and resilience will help you navigate your way out of erratic growth spurts and into a life that reaches its full potential. Without these growth attitudes, you'll constantly struggle with your personal development. But with them, you're poised for a personal growth revolution.

PART TWO

The Five Levels of
Personal Growth

Chapter 3

The Learning Level: Choosing Growth

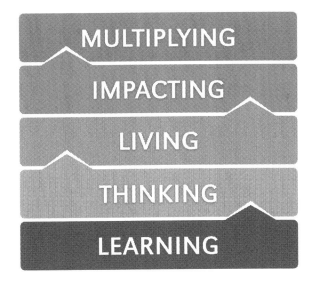

G od is telling a grand story—in fact, He has been telling that story ever since the creation. His story is filled with the beauty of Eden, the tragedy of Egyptian slavery, the awe of the parting of the Red Sea, and the glory of the Promised Land. His story drips with the blood of the cross and soars with the triumph of the resurrection. His story is good news.

The story God is writing features prostitutes, tax collectors, shepherds, kings, priests, fishermen, murderers, liars, and adulterers. It includes inventors, mechanics, builders, poets, and politicians. It has executives, engineers, nurses, musicians, athletes, and teachers. It features moms, dads, sons, and daughters. God's story includes...you.

God's story continues, and we each have a role. You could be an understudy or a headliner, but most of us settle for being extras or even worse, scenery. The Apostle Paul understood the importance of taking your place in God's story when he wrote, "I, Paul, have been sent on special assignment by Christ as part of God's master plan."[8] He recognized that God has a master plan and that He's invited us to play a part in it.

So what does God's story have to do with starting a personal growth revolution? And why bring it up now, at the Learning Level—the first level—of personal growth? Because all learning has a driver, and what drives your learning profoundly shapes the person you become in God's story.

What's Driving Your Learning?

Everybody would agree that learning is essential to life. But *lifelong learning* is a different story. How many times have you learned for the sake of *getting by* rather than *getting better?* Between these two mentalities is the war zone where you'll either win or lose your battle for lifelong learning. When you learn enough to get by—graduating school, getting a job, no longer leeching off mom and dad—it's easy to start thinking, "That's enough, I don't need to get any better." That approach to learning is ultimately driven by mediocrity—an attitude of mental laziness that blocks the road to your personal growth.

Mediocrity-driven learning carries with it an unintended consequence—irrelevance. American social writer Eric Hoffer observed, "In times of change, learners inherit the earth, while the learned find themselves beautifully equipped to deal with a world that no longer exists."

> "In times of change, learners inherit the earth, while the learned find themselves beautifully equipped to deal with a world that no longer exists."

When mediocrity drives your learning, the focus is always on reaching a single goal. Once you've achieved the goal, you conveniently stop learning and start coasting on the momentum of your prior experience. You may not decide to start growing again until you find yourself outdated, and experiencing firsthand the pain of irrelevance. When that happens, your commitment to learning is reactive—you only do it when your environment demands that you grow and change to survive.

But there's a much better type of learning. It's a kind of learning that helps you not only close your growth gaps, but helps you do so while being cognizant of God's work in and around you. As I shared in the first chapter, God created us with a specific capacity, and between our present state and our full capacity is a gap. That gap is our growth potential. But let me take that concept one step further. Your gap is more than your growth potential...it's your *missional potential.* Your missional potential is where God's mission intersects your growth gap. *In other words, your focus shouldn't be to reach your potential so*

> Your missional potential is where God's mission intersects your growth gap.

that you can achieve your own selfish goals. Your focus should be to reach your potential in such a way that God's mission is advanced in and through your life.

This brings God into the equation of your growth. This makes you sensitive to the story God is telling, and helps you proactively seek out learning opportunities that will help you better play your part in His story. When your learning is driven by your missional potential—rather than mediocrity—you'll discover a purpose for your growth that is much bigger than yourself. Suddenly growth takes on eternal significance rather than being centered on selfish ambitions.

Mediocrity vs. Missional Potential

Mediocrity focuses on short-term personal gains. Missional potential asks, "How can I grow long-term?" and "What contribution will my growth make?" One centers on what you can *get* while the other concentrates on what you can *give*. One makes you a lazy learner while the other prods you to be a lifelong learner.

Learning as a way to fulfill your missional potential is always proactive—you *choose* to learn constantly, consistently, strategically, and intentionally in partnership with the work that God's doing. This partnership keeps your focus on the person God has called you to become and the difference He has called you to make. The following chart contrasts the differences in learning driven by mediocrity versus missional potential.

——— LEARNING DRIVEN BY ———

MEDIOCRITY	MISSIONAL POTENTIAL
Learning to get by	Learning to get better
Learning for the sake of survival and short-term gains	Learning for long-term growth and contribution
Learning that's reactive	Learning that's proactive
Learning focused on my personal ambitions	Learning in step with God's mission in me and around me

The driving force behind your learning is a choice that you have to make. If mediocrity is your choice, you'll never close your growth gaps. But if you choose your missional potential to sit in the driver's seat of your personal growth, you'll go farther than you ever dreamed possible. Which will you choose—mediocrity or missional potential?

The Apostle Paul chose his missional potential to be his personal growth driver. He embraced his special assignment and walked in step with God's master plan. This wasn't a feel-good decision made in a moment of euphoria. It was a decision that Paul took to heart right up to the end of his life.

In his second letter to Timothy, as he was nearing death, Paul celebrated the fact that he had fought the good fight, finished the race, and kept the faith.[9] Then he made a special request: "Bring the winter coat I left in Troas with Carpus; also the books and parchment notebooks."[10] When most people near the end of life, their final requests ease their regrets, restore their relationships, or comfort their weakening bodies. But not Paul! He refused to toss learning in the backseat just because his days were numbered. His *books* were among his final requests. Lifelong learning, driven by his missional potential, didn't relinquish the driver's seat until Paul drew his last breath.

Don't let excuses paralyze you; refuse to be a reactive learner. Don't wait for your life and circumstances to force you to grow. Too much is at stake—the very work God wants to do inside and around you—to let mediocrity dictate your learning. Proactive learning is an internal and intentional decision—one that requires you to draw a line in the sand and boldly declare, "From this day forward my learning will be driven by my missional potential!"

Characteristics of the Learning Level

Learning is the foundation of the five levels of personal growth. Without learning, you simply cannot grow. It's your starting point. It's the skill that precedes all others. So how do you develop this skill in your life? How do you know when you've reached the Learning Level of personal growth? Three characteristics will be obvious in your life: A decision to grow, a direction for growth, and a diet for growth.

A DECISION TO GROW

When I was in high school I made the *wrong* choice—I only learned when I had to, and just enough to get by. The only thing I went out of my way to learn was shortcuts. I didn't cheat, but I also didn't apply myself. I was typically content with Bs and Cs (even the occasional D or F). I rarely put in the time or effort to do better. One reason was that I hated reading. It didn't matter what kind of reading—novel, history book, short story—reading was not my thing. Unlike my wife, who grew up with a steady diet of books, I restricted my reading to *TV Guide*. Reading drained me. And most of what I read was boring.

College could have opened my eyes to reading, but no way I was going to let that happen. Throughout most of college, I only cracked half of my textbooks. (Nothing like spending dad's money to buy books you never read.) It wasn't that I *couldn't* read—I just didn't *like* to. Turns out, I wasn't alone. Only 45% of Americans over the age of 13 read a book in the course of a year.[11]

After graduating college with all the answers, it took me a couple of years to realize just how little I actually knew. In fact, those first two years of ministry were...how should I say this?... an experiment in stupidity. I alienated people, made dumb decisions, had a negative attitude, and was extremely naïve. Once my pastor tried to buy me a book on attitude. Ironically, I was offended. As if all those things weren't enough, I once burned a hole in a church pew with a flash pot gone bad—less than 12 months after we had just remodeled the auditorium. Forrest Gump's famous words encapsulated my life: "Stupid is as stupid does."

When I finally realized how well prepared I was for irrelevance, that newfound humility forced me into a learning mode. In the years that followed—mostly out of necessity—I developed a habit of reading. At first it was slow and inconsistent. I'd pick up a book here or there and occasionally read a magazine article. I can still remember reading John Maxwell's early leadership book, *Developing the Leader Within You*, and thinking, "This is the best leadership book I've ever read." Suddenly it occurred to me: "This is the *only* leadership book I've ever read."

But that book, along with others, was a spark that ignited the Learning Level of personal growth in my professional life.

A subtle, but powerful, revolution had begun. I made a *decision* to grow. I took to heart the words of Mark Twain: "The man who does not read good books has no advantage over the man who cannot read them." And I discovered a simple truth—with every page I read, my appetite for personal growth grew.

Today I'm an avid reader, but more importantly, I'm a lifelong learner. I made a *decision* to let my missional potential drive my learning, and then I followed that decision with one baby growth step after another. What about you? Would the people who know you well describe you with the phrase "lifelong learner"? If not, that can change. But you have to make a decision to grow.

As simple as it sounds, many people never make that decision. It won't happen if you just wait for life and your circumstances to *demand* that you grow—like I did when I started in ministry. Mediocrity is tempting, because it's easy to just take a seat in someone else's ride and let your potential lie dormant inside of you. But if you choose to cruise through life in the passenger seat, learning only when you *have* to, then your growth won't be on your terms. To truly grow into your potential, you have to decide to pick out your own car and head out onto the open road. That's where the action is.

The true test of whether your decision sticks will be the behavior that follows it. But you won't start until you first make a clear-cut, uncompromised decision. Revolutions start with "Go!" Your life today is the sum total of all your decisions. That means that your decision about personal growth today will greatly determine your life tomorrow.

Don't take this decision lightly. And once you've made it, you'll still have to manage it daily. Growth is a posture, not just a phase you go through. A phase lasts for a season and then it's over. But a posture is an attitude. Your decision to grow is more than a single act of growth—it's a frame of mind and a lifestyle of continual improvement.

So, let me ask you one more time—*have you made that choice?* Have you decided to become a lifelong learner, to set aside the "easy" life of mediocrity and grow to your full missional potential? If you haven't, please set this book down right now and make your choice. Don't just flirt with the decision—marry it!

A DIRECTION FOR GROWTH

Once you've settled the decision, you need to set a course. Not surprisingly, the *direction* you choose for your journey is your compass. Author and Harvard Business School professor John Kotter once observed, "Most people don't lead their own lives—they accept their lives." Leading your life always begins when you determine where you want to go with your life. In other words, where do you want to lead your life *to*? Or better yet, what direction does *God* want to lead your life *in*?

So how do you find direction for your growth? It's simple: **who you desire to become and what you desire to do gives direction to where and how you need to grow.** Discovering your "be/do" capacity helps you figure out both the level at which you're currently functioning as well as what potential you still have remaining. The gap between those two reveals your growth course. That growth course will develop over time, and as we'll see in the next chapter, you can create a fresh growth course every year (or even every few months) to keep your growth focused and vibrant.

I was out of school for 15 years when I chose a growth course to pursue a master's degree. Many people don't return to school because they say, "It's too late," "What's the point?" or "It'll take too long." But as a friend of mine once said, "Stephen, you can be 42 years old *with* a master's degree or 42 years old *without* a master's degree. Either way, one day you'll be 42 years old."

Going back to school was one of many growth courses I've chosen based on my understanding of my growth gaps and my missional potential. I came to realize that there's no such thing as "too late" or "too long" when you're a lifelong learner. And if you think you're too old to learn something new, consider the story of Jim Henry from Connecticut. Jim's father pulled him out of school as a young boy so he could help support his family. As a result, he was illiterate most of his life...until his *mid-nineties* when he finally learned how to read. He was so excited by his learning journey that he wrote and published a book when he was 98 years old. It's never too late to explore new territory in your learning journey.

Every day is just another day of learning (and growing). The key is to keep choosing a direction for your growth that closes your growth gaps and moves you further toward your full capacity. When you do, personal growth takes on a unique quality that makes it just like money earning interest in the bank: it compounds over time.

A DIET FOR GROWTH

If making your decision to grow is the key to the car, and if choosing a direction to grow is your compass, then figuring out your diet for growth is the gas you put in your tank. If you don't know how to fill your tank and keep it topped off, you're in for a short trip. Your journey will be limited by the person you are today. Learning happens when the fuel you put in your growth tank works together with the decision you make and the direction you choose. What you have in your tank—and how often you refuel—determines how far you can go.

One day you'll look back over your life and see just how far you've come. That moment will be the first time you can fully realize the true capacity God created within you. Unfortunately, some people won't get to experience the joy of reflecting on a lifetime of learning. Instead, they'll reach the end of a life of lazy living, wondering "what could have been" as they reflect into a rearview mirror filled with regrets. The problem wasn't their God-given capacity, it was their lack of discipline to grow intentionally (and daily) by selecting the right growth diet. (We'll talk in more specifics about what to put in your growth tank in the next chapter.)

It's Time

Have you arrived at the Learning Level? Have you made the *decision* to be a lifelong learner? That decision will be the defining moment that you come back to time and again, especially when you feel like coasting. How about your direction and diet for growth? Are you ready to choose your course and start filling your tank? These are the characteristics of the Learning Level, and in the next chapter we'll grab hold of the first practice of the five levels of personal growth—the key to launching the Learning Level. It's time!

---- *Chapter 4* ----

Growth TRACing: Closing Your Growth Gaps

"**Y**ou make me feel underappreciated and you push for too much progress." That was the message Jeff heard loud and clear from his administrative assistant. Jeff is a focused, strategic, high-capacity leader, and a high-achiever who can never be accused of taking it easy at work. So when Allison confronted him about his hard-charging leadership style, it revealed a growth gap, and in Jeff's words, "it surfaced a pretty big lack of awareness in me about the way I interacted with people that I was leading on a team." From Jeff's point of view, he was setting Allison up to succeed and feel empowered. But from Allison's point of view, Jeff was pulling the plug on her emotional gas tank.

Many leaders in Jeff's shoes would power up and tell their assistant to toughen up, take initiative, and get on board. But that's exactly the kind of behavior that causes the problem in the first place. So Jeff took a different route. He created a personal growth plan to help him develop his emotional intelligence—an essential leadership competency in today's work environment.

Initially his plan was pretty basic: Read a book on emotional intelligence and put the principles in the book to work. So Jeff plunged into the material and put together a practical road-map. Step-by-step, he made progress. But his growth wasn't enough. The gap needed more attention. So, two years later, Jeff refocused on his growth goal, beefed up his growth plan, and upped the ante on his accountability. He read another book on emotional intelligence, found a mentor to help him accel-erate his progress, and drafted a one-page emotional intelli-gence leadership plan to help him stay focused on the right things. Even after seeing measurable progress, Jeff was still eager to grow. So he pushed himself by taking an intensive training course on emotional intelligence.

Today, Jeff's growth is producing remarkable results. He regularly receives positive feedback. In fact, his last two 360-de-gree evaluations at work revealed that making others feel em-powered, encouraged, and supported are among his strongest traits. Reflecting on his growth, Jeff says, "What I learned was that my strengths of drive, focus, and achieving just overpow-ered the other stuff. So now I'm able to temper those strengths because I'm very self aware about them. I've learned to solicit a lot of feedback about how I'm coming across. I also had to learn a few simple habits to get into my routine." Because Jeff kept learning and growing, today he's certified to administer an assessment and provide helpful coaching to others who want to grow in their emotional intelligence too.

Jeff's growth process began when he became aware of his growth gap. Unfortunately that's where too many people end their growth journey. But Jeff didn't. He took the next step and created a growth plan that included resources, a mentoring and accountability relationship, practical application ideas, and intensive training. As a result, Jeff experienced the power of personal growth to transform his performance at work. He successfully avoided "the resolution ritual" that so many people experience at the start of a new year.

The Resolution Ritual

"Happy New Year!" When you hear someone say that, what comes to your mind? Chances are, besides picturing silly hats, noisemakers, people in heavy coats, glitter and confetti, you also think of *resolutions*. Many of us look to the final days of a year as an excuse to binge (even if it's only a little) confident that in that first day of the new year, we'll make our fresh start.

New Year's resolutions are common around the world. In fact, most "top ten lists" for New Year's resolutions look a lot like this:

1. Lose weight
2. Stick to a budget
3. Reduce debt
4. Spend more time with family and friends
5. Quit smoking
6. Fall in love
7. Enjoy life more
8. Learn something new
9. Volunteer or help others
10. Get organized

If you're in the ritual of setting New Year's resolutions, there's a good chance at least one of these ten made your list. And as Dr. Phil might say, "How's that workin' for ya?" Have you made any progress? Did you start strong but now you're wallowing in defeat? If so, don't feel bad. You're certainly not alone. In fact, only 8% of Americans say they always achieve their New Year's resolutions...and three out of four almost never succeed.[12]

But is "setting goals" really the problem? The only thing a New Year's resolution or growth goal is really good for is a destination—preferably one aligned with your missional potential, of course. But that's not enough. You also need a *track* you can run on—a way to jumpstart the Learning Level with a realistic path toward your destination. That's what Jeff did... and that brings us to the first practice of the five levels of personal growth.

GO! Practice #1: Growth TRACing: How to Move to the Learning Level

Every level of personal growth has the ability to foster life change. Each one is a powerful force that can turbocharge your missional potential, close your capacity gaps, and help you impact not only yourself, but also the people you influence. Each level needs a unique practice—what I call a *GO! Practice*—to give it its power for change, and each of those practices generates a specific *outcome*. These outcomes cluster together, eventually exploding exponentially as amazing transformation in your life.

There's one practice that will activate the Learning Level of personal growth faster than any other: Growth TRACing (pronounced "tracking"). A Growth TRAC is how you create, implement, and then monitor your own plan for personal growth. Your Growth TRAC gives you the structure you'll need to measure your progress so you can actually "see" your goals and dreams approaching as you get closer to them. It's like the framework of your personal growth revolution. You may be thinking, "No! I *hate* structure and routine!" That's fine. I'll tell you later how to use your unique personality type to shape a Growth TRAC that works specifically for you. In fact, as you begin to discover your own learning style and approach, you'll see that a Growth TRAC is a powerful component to your learning journey.

Why a Growth **TRAC** Makes Sense

For years, organizations have tried to tell their employees "how" to grow so they could accelerate their job performance. Schools have adopted one-size-fits-all academic tracks to get students to achieve the degrees the school wants them to have. Churches have aggressively expanded their programs (rather than actually developing people). All of these approaches eat up funding and staffing, and yet may not even help the people they're trying to reach.

Reggie McNeal, author and Missional Leadership Specialist for Leadership Network, makes a poignant observation about how our own history led us into this predicament in the church:

> ...the rise of the program-driven church correlates directly with the rise of the service economy in post-World War II America. The manufacturing engine powering the economy yielded to the service sector as Americans could afford to pay other people to do things they no longer wanted to do themselves or couldn't do themselves. People began to outsource food preparation, lawn maintenance, laundry, oil changes, and child care. And Americans outsourced spiritual formation to the church. It was during this period that the concept of church as a vendor of religious goods

and services became entrenched in the ethos of the North American church culture.[13]

McNeal further explains that people began looking to the church as the place where they could "live out their entire spiritual journey as part of a church-sponsored or church-operated activity." Well, "the times they are a-changing" (again). Emerging generations, advances in technology, and the realization that a one-size-fits-all approach doesn't fit everyone, after all, are changing the dynamics of personal growth. If you're going to develop your full missional potential, you'll need a customized TRAC that takes into account the unique identity God placed within you.

So, how does a Growth TRAC help you reach the Learning Level of personal growth? And what does Growth TRACing look like? You need four essential components for an airtight, personalized, missionally-sensitive TRAC. Each component answers an important growth question:[14]

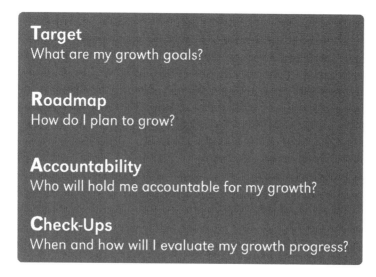

Target
What are my growth goals?

Roadmap
How do I plan to grow?

Accountability
Who will hold me accountable for my growth?

Check-Ups
When and how will I evaluate my growth progress?

TARGET: WHAT ARE MY GROWTH GOALS?

You have to start a healthy Growth TRAC by figuring out in which areas you need to grow in the first place. Assessing that will help you set goals, or *targets*. These targets will become your "true north" as you lay out the rest of your Growth TRAC. Now, setting a target may seem really straightforward and obvious, but in my experience, most people misunderstand this task.

It's easy to look at our growth gaps (particularly our weaknesses) and say, "That's where I need to grow." In fact, we often tend to think about our personal growth as a way to mitigate or overcome our weaknesses. For example, when you receive a performance review at work, it typically highlights your shortcomings. You and your boss then use those weaknesses as the baseline to identify which things you should focus on improving. However, comprehensive research has strongly suggested—perhaps counter-intuitively—that your greatest potential for growth is actually in your areas of greatest strength, *not* in your weaknesses.[15] Figure 1 explains the difference between strengths, weaknesses, and liabilities and their role in personal growth.

Figure 1
Strengths, Weaknesses, Liabilities

After surveying more than 1.7 million employees in large companies around the world, the Gallup Organization discovered that only 20 percent of employees have the opportunity to do what they do best every day. Further study revealed that most organizations are only operating at 20 percent capacity. So what causes this way-too-common capacity gap? Gallup's research determined that most organizations are built on two flawed assumptions. First, each person can learn to be competent in almost anything; and second, each person's best indicators for growth are in the areas where they're the weakest.

Ironically, although this represents the traditional thinking about weaknesses, it actually has the opposite effect of what's intended. What is supposed to liberate you and make you "better" ends up being a set of shackles. I'm not suggesting that we should ignore our weaknesses. What I am saying is that we often do just that with our strengths. **Your best strategy is one that builds on your strengths, manages your weaknesses, and addresses your liabilities.**

Strengths are the areas where you demonstrate gifting, natural talent, passion, and successfully learned skills. It's through your strengths that you will make your greatest contribution to your job, community, and society at large. Your strengths—which God placed within you in the first place, by the way—are what He will most consistently use to serve His mission in the world. That's precisely why you should grow your strengths to the highest levels possible.

Weaknesses, on the other hand, are those areas where God did not gift you, perhaps at all. For me "the short list" includes things like music, sports, mechanics, carpentry, science, math, and counseling (although I could go on pretty much indefinitely). I am miserably bad at all of these things. But there's a reason God didn't gift me with these abilities: He didn't need me to have them! The slice of God's mission where He called me to serve doesn't require that I excel in these areas. The appropriate response to weaknesses is to manage the ones that are most necessary in everyday life. For example, although you might not be good at finances, you still need to acquire enough knowledge about managing your money so that you don't wind up buried under a mountain of debt.

Liabilities are any behaviors, attitudes, or personality traits that cause (or could lead to) neglect in key areas of your life, prevent the fulfillment of God's purpose for your life, or sabotage your character, integrity, or relationships. These are more than weaknesses—they're inherent disadvantages that have the potential to derail your life. You cannot ignore character flaws, your family and friends, a relationship with God, your physical, emotional, and financial health, or any other area necessary for you to fulfill your missional potential. Your liabilities are diabolical enemies. Ignoring them will result in certain disappointment and devastation. Compensating for them will keep you in the game.

You'll need to set the targets of your Growth TRAC on both extremes: building on your strengths while at the same time addressing (at least some of) your liabilities. The key is not to give your weaknesses undue attention. You should manage them at a basic level—just enough to keep them from hurting your life or hindering your potential.

So what kind of targets should you include in your Growth TRAC? Luke 2:52 offers us a pretty good template to start from. The Bible says, "Jesus grew in wisdom and stature, and in favor with God and men." Jesus set focused, intentional, and balanced growth targets for himself. You need to do that, too. Here are some key areas that your TRAC should target:

- **Spiritual Growth.** Address your relationship with God, spiritual disciplines, and your character formation.
- **Mental Growth.** Address your gifts, abilities, skills, passions, emotions, responsibilities, and life purpose.
- **Relational Growth.** Address your relationships with friends, family, neighbors, co-workers, Christ-followers, and those exploring spirituality.
- **Physical Growth.** Address areas of nutrition, fitness, and health.

These four broad categories provide language for your growth gaps and will help you pinpoint the targets for your Growth TRAC. You may have strengths or liabilities within each of these areas. (For a list of recommended assessments to help you gauge your health in key growth areas, turn to Appendix A.) As you identify your growth targets, strike a balance between your strengths and your liabilities. Furthermore, limit how many growth goals you tackle at once. Don't pursue more than 3-6 growth targets during any 6-12 month period of time. You have a lifetime to grow...don't try to squeeze it all into one year.

ROADMAP: HOW DO I PLAN TO GROW?

Identifying your targets is only the first step of your Growth TRAC. Your targets will give you a destination and point you in the right direction. Your next step is to create a unique *roadmap*, one that will specifically lead you to each of your targets. As you plot your growth roadmap in each of your target areas, make sure it routes through these four service stations: *training, resources, relationships,* and *experiences*.

Training means any kind of education you can get, whether classes, schooling, conferences, seminars, workshops, or other instructional opportunities. In-depth training can be extremely valuable in your ongoing growth process. I've seen people make major changes in their behavior (and even habits) after participating in a training course that required outside personal study or homework. Look for courses that pair inspirational content with teaching that shows you how to meaningfully apply that inspiration directly into your daily life.

You'll find many events designed to improve performance; however, be aware that change does not happen *at* large training events. Events inspire change. Process creates change. Habits sustain change. An event can give you a lot of useful ideas. But following the event, you'll still need to pass through the other three stops on your roadmap—resources, relationships, and experiences. As you collect souvenirs from each of these, they will come together to produce change within you, and new habits will form. These habits will sustain your personal growth over time.

> *Events inspire change.*
> *Process creates change.*
> *Habits sustain change.*

Resources can include books, magazines, CDs, DVDs, assessments, podcasts, blogs, web-based tools, and any other media that transports new ideas for life change into your mind. The idea of accessing resources to stimulate growth is nothing new. Author Zig Ziglar used to talk about "the automobile university" for years. While serving as a visiting scholar at the University of Southern California for two years, Ziglar learned of a study indicating the growth potential you can realize while driving. USC discovered that people living in a metropolitan area who drive a minimum of 12,000 miles per year could acquire the equivalent of two years of college education in just three years, simply by turning their car into an educational environment.

Ziglar once offered his executive assistant as a perfect example. She only finished the tenth grade, but was the best assistant Ziglar ever had. Every day on her way to and from the office, she listened to personal growth resources in her car. Besides that, she became a prolific reader and was always on the lookout for opportunities to grow. After having herself evaluated, she tested at a level slightly above a Master's degree. How did she get there? She made a deep commitment to learning and acquired the resources she needed to grow.[16]

How are you leveraging your daily commute for personal growth? A Gallup survey[17] revealed that the average American worker spends 46 minutes per day commuting round trip to work. Do the math. That's an average of 230 minutes per week, over 15 hours per month, and nearly 200 hours per year. Rather than just using that time to get yourself from point A to point B, why not use it to get your mind from point A to point B by listening to podcasts, teachings, interviews, and books?

Relationships are the third stop in your roadmap. While you'll need to stop at all four stations on your roadmap to fill up along the way, relationships hold arguably the most potential bang for your buck. Relationships can include discipling, coaching, mentoring, counseling, and personal friendships. Take coaching for example. We're all familiar with the idea of coaching in sports, but often we overlook it in other areas of our lives.

A coach helps you maximize your potential by asking questions to assess your aspirations and obstacles, drawing out breakthrough insights that will help you grow, and helping you translate these insights into practical action steps. Coaches also stand on the sidelines to cheer you on, motivating and encouraging you on your journey.

The coaches in your life help you see both sides of the learning coin. Mark Batterson, pastor of the multi-site National Community Church in Washington, D.C., put it simply: "Half of learning is learning. The other half of learning is unlearning." Coaches help you accomplish both—unlearning bad thinking and learning best practices. Tom Landry, the highly respected legendary coach of the Dallas Cowboys, once observed, "A coach is someone who tells you what you don't want to hear and has you see what you don't want to see, so that you can be who you've always known you could be."

> "Half of learning is learning. The other half of learning is unlearning."[8]

Several years ago, I asked a wise coworker if he would coach me through writing a life mission statement for myself. Thankfully, he agreed. The process was exhilarating. He helped me reflect on my strengths, pinpoint my passions, and uncover the seeds of destiny that God had already been planting in me throughout my life. What emerged was a single, focused, powerfully motivating sentence that helps me stay focused on my mission in life:

My mission is to lead, coach, and equip leaders and churches to engage in the process of personal growth, develop their full leadership capacity, and produce effective, kingdom-advancing ministry.

Without his patient coaching, there's no way I would have been able to articulate my purpose with such clarity.

Connect with people who can help you strategically move forward in the growth areas you've targeted. Some will be personal friends or close family members. Others will be professional coaches or counselors. Some might be spiritual leaders or excellent coworkers. Ask yourself, "Who do I already know who can help me grow?" If you honestly can't think of anybody, then ask yourself, "What do I need to do to start connecting with the right people, people who can help me meet my growth needs?"

Experiences are the last essential stop on the roadmap of your Growth TRAC. Experiences include any opportunities, activities, or assignments that directly stimulate your growth. For example, if you need to get in better physical health, you first identify that as a growth target, then add an activity to your roadmap: "Join a health club" or "Schedule a physical with my doctor." If you want to further your education, add an assignment to your roadmap: "Research local school programs" or "Register for X courses," where X is the topic you'd like to learn more about. If you want your roadmap to lead you into a deeper relationship with God, then add something like: "Schedule spiritual retreat," "Volunteer for Y community service project," or "Sign up for Z mission trip." All of these—activities, assignments, and opportunities—qualify as experiences.

Training, resources, relationships, and experiences are an integral part of the highway system that makes up countless personal growth roadmaps. Take George Washington, for example. His roadmap included training in military history and economics, a library collection of 734 books, mentors who helped him refine his skills in surveying, math, and geography, and experiences such as keeping a diary—a habit he started when he was 16 and continued for the rest of his life. (Today, this amazing compilation of history occupies 163 linear feet of shelving in the Library of Congress.)

Washington's roadmap for growth shaped his leadership as the Commander in Chief of the Continental Army during the American Revolution and, of course, as the first President of the United States. Clearly, a roadmap is an important part of your Growth TRAC.

ACCOUNTABILITY: WHO WILL HOLD ME ACCOUNTABLE FOR MY GROWTH?

Accountability is perhaps the most emotional, most intense part of a Growth TRAC. We all need it, but few of us want it. Accountability can be automated or customized.

Automated accountability is just that—automatic. You don't get a say, and the expectations on you are clear. When you were a kid, your parents probably gave you certain chores around the house. You didn't get a vote. They were *your* chores and *your* responsibility, period. If Mondays and Thursdays were trash days, you were *expected* to take out the trash. (And if you didn't, you'd face certain, probably specific, consequences.) Accountability was automatic. When you get a new job, HR typically doesn't ask you if you want taxes taken out of your payroll. Instead, they just ask, "How much do you want taken out?" Paying taxes is required, and the IRS holds you accountable if you don't pay. Again, the accountability is automatic—you have no choice in the matter.

Customized accountability is different. While everybody is subject to automatic accountability, very few of us pursue customized accountability. Customized accountability means actively seeking out accountability partners for each target you've set in your Growth TRAC. Customized accountability is difficult because it's personal. When, in an effort to cultivate purity in your life, you ask someone to hold you accountable for the websites you view online, you've just given them permission to get into your personal space. You're not just taking the trash out on Mondays and Thursdays; now you're giving someone permission to see what's inside your trash bags.

Customized accountability also exposes the real you. It's easy to put on a mask that covers the dark closets of your mind, but the fundamental foundation of accountability is truthfulness and transparency. If you can't be honest about who you really are, then you can't grow into the person God has called you to become. Transparency means you can't candy-coat your answers to an accountability partner's tough questions. Genuine transparency gets to know the truth—the good, the bad, and the ugly.

This entire accountability process takes a deep level of trust. Sharing your struggles is tough. It's a blow to your pride. Finding the right person to share them with is even tougher. Typically, you should select an accountability partner who "matches" a specific type of growth goal you've set for yourself. For example, for a spiritual growth target, you might ask a pastor, mentor, or prayer partner to hold you accountable. If you've set a physical growth goal, get a workout partner (a tough one, preferably one who's already achieved what you're aiming for). If your target is to grow mentally, ask a teacher, counselor, coworker, or advisor to be an accountability partner. If you set a relational growth goal, your spouse, a close friend, or a relative might be willing to help you.

Draw from your current pool of relationships, and let your growth target tell you who your accountability partner should be. Once you've established accountability, create standing appointments with each partner. Whether you meet every Thursday morning over coffee or every first Monday of the month for lunch, intentionally make accountability a regular part of your routine. I easily neglect my own accountability unless I'm diligent to schedule it as appointments. I have to make myself meet every week with an accountability partner, or I'll simply never "get around to it." I build it into my schedule. I've found that's the only way I can stay on track with my growth targets. Do what you have to do to make these happen.

CHECK-UPS: WHEN AND HOW WILL I EVALUATE MY GROWTH PROGRESS?

The fourth component of your Growth TRAC is one that you'll revisit multiple times during the process. Remember when we talked about New Year's resolutions? Have you ever set a growth goal at the beginning of the year, only to be sorely disappointed in yourself at the end of the year (when you finally remembered it again)? In January, you were excited to choose your growth target and draft your roadmap. But by the time Thanksgiving rolled around, you realized you were defeated. "How can I possibly reach this goal in the last 30 days of the year? I give up!" Typically, the problem is not with your growth goal; it's that you didn't build check-ups into your growth cycle. If you don't check your growth weekly, monthly, or quarterly, you won't keep your priorities set, and your growth targets will slip.

Before you wrap up the details of your Growth TRAC, determine *how* and schedule *when* you'll evaluate your progress. Begin by developing a clear timeline for every growth step in your Growth TRAC. Put your action steps from your roadmap directly into your daily schedule. John Maxwell says that your success is determined by your daily agenda. How you spend your time makes things happen (or not happen) and defines who you do (or don't) become.

If you plan to read a book, set a start date and an end date. If you're going to meet with a financial advisor, decide what date and time you'll actually call to set the appointment. If you plan to go on a family vacation, write the dates when you're going (and when you'll have the money saved to pay for it). Creating a timeline for each action step helps you pace yourself throughout the year. Your timeline helps you manage your tasks, so you won't try to do too much at one time. Timelines also help you assess how long it will take you to complete each growth goal. When every step of your roadmap is on your schedule, your calendar automatically reminds you when it's time to work on a step. This allows you to forget about your Growth TRAC... without forgetting to grow.

Once you've created a timeline for your Growth TRAC and posted each growth step on your calendar, schedule progress evaluation meetings with your accountability partners. While accountability is the "A" in your Growth TRAC, it also plays an important role in check-ups. Progress evaluations lean on accountability partners to reflect on an extended period of time (say 3-6 months) to look for measurable progress. These evaluations are good mid-course check-ups to help you gain perspective and make necessary adjustments.

You might look at the Growth TRAC model above and say to yourself, "I can't do this! I'm not structured enough. I hate routine. I'm too spontaneous to follow a rigid growth plan. My personality just doesn't have enough *planner* in it to follow a Growth TRAC." Actually, that's the beauty of this model. **Any personality type can use the Growth TRAC because it's built around a set of questions. Your personality will—and should—dictate how you answer those questions.** Appendix B offers some helpful insight on the different learning styles of each personality type and how your personality should shape your Growth TRAC.

From Growth **TRAC**ing to Growth Traction

Growth TRACing is the GO! PRACTICE of the Learning Level of personal growth. Growth TRACing gives you structure, direction, accountability, and practical action steps. (See appendix C for sample Growth TRACs and a Growth TRAC template.)

The OUTCOME of Growth TRACing is growth traction. If you just "do stuff" randomly towards a goal, rather than actually TRACing it, you might just be spinning your wheels. But when you combine a Growth TRAC with growth action, you achieve growth traction. Growth TRACing is the practice that produces your traction...which carries you to the progress you wanted in the first place. You'll discover deep fulfillment as you begin to notice positive changes spiritually, mentally, relationally, and physically. But you know what's most rewarding about the traction that Growth TRACing produces? The person it shapes you into is closer to your God-given potential.

Your personal growth can have massive positive impact not only on your own life, but also on the lives of those you love, care about, and influence. Try to picture some of the results and benefits of having invested the "appropriate" number of hours into your personal development. Step-by-step, your growth gaps will begin to close. You'll draw closer and closer to your full, God-given capacity.

Philosopher, author, and radio host Earl Nightingale once said, "If a person will spend one hour a day on the same subject for five years, that person will be an expert on that subject." Further research suggests that it takes an average of 2.7 hours of practice per day (over a ten year period) to develop the highest levels of expertise in a subject. That's roughly 10,000 hours of practice. But when you consistently engage the Growth TRACing process, that, and more, is possible. Growth TRACing initiates the Learning Level, and you create genuine traction in the areas that are the most important to you.

Go! Get started. Today. Seriously. Create your *own* Growth TRAC. Appendices A, B, and C will help you. Plan some time to design a TRAC to intentionally accelerate your personal growth. Don't just dream about the person you want to become. Don't just imagine the revolution that can take place inside of you. Build your own TRAC to make it happen. That's what Jeff did when he faced his own emotional intelligence growth gap. He drafted a specific plan to grow and made the future he wanted into a reality. And so can you. This single step will activate the Learning Level in your life and launch a growth revolution like you've never seen before.

Blindsided by Personal Growth

Before I wrap up this chapter, I need to make one final point: not all growth is planned...it can blindside you, too. Growth doesn't always fit neatly into your Growth TRAC. Some growth is like being dealt a personal growth wildcard that you never asked for. Sometimes—in fact, many times—growth opportunities *come to you*. They don't wait for you to pursue them; they pursue you.

Some of these growth opportunities are masked as tests of integrity, unexpected trials, disappointments, poor job reviews, attitude checks, wake-up calls about your health, or even interactions with people who just rub you the wrong way. Other growth opportunities come out of left field as pleasant surprises...your pastor unexpectedly invites you to serve in a role that taps your gifts and abilities for Kingdom purposes; your boss invites you to a high-end training experience; the door opens to move into your dream job; or your spouse surprises you and your kids with a great family outing. Regardless of the source, you should be committed to growth...period.

The Learning Level is about more than the growth that you intentionally go after (using your Growth TRAC as your guide). It's also about the growth that chases you...the growth that you're not always excited about but is just as essential to your development. Either way, your job is to keep your personal growth antenna up and tuned in to the learning opportunities around you. A personal growth opportunity might blindside you, but don't let it go to waste. Capture it. Learn from it. Grow because of it.

Nothing Can Stop You Now...But You

The Learning Level of personal growth is your launch pad. God deposited your mission within you. Consciously cultivate the health you need in those strategic areas of your life to propel yourself upward. Now you have the step-by-step process to create your own Growth TRAC. Use that to catalyze your Learning Level. The ball's in your court. It's your move. It's time to GO. Develop your Growth TRAC. Find your Growth Traction. Don't waste growth opportunities. Get started, and you'll be well on your way to the next level of personal growth...*Thinking.*

GO! Starting a Personal Growth Revolution				
GO! Practice	Activates	Level of Personal Growth	Which results in	Outcome
Growth TRACing	⟶	The Learning Level	⟶	Growth Traction

—— *Chapter 5* ——

The Thinking Level:
Play-Doh and Seesaws

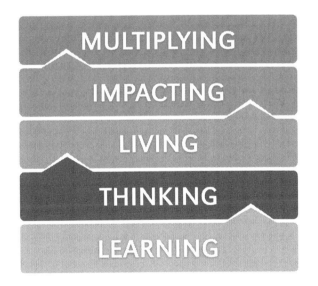

W hen you were a kid, there's a good chance you took an art class in school—maybe even several art classes. Art was always a fun class because your mind could race with creativity as your hands turned your imagination into a "work of art"—if that's what you can call a five-year-old's creation. So what did you love about art? Most kids are naturally inclined to make a mess, so maybe painting caught your eye. After all, anything gooey with the ability to leave a permanent stain has to be fun, right? Or perhaps the fat crayons were calling your name. Bright, colorful, and too big to get lodged in your nose, they were the starter pack until you could graduate to the 64-count jumbo box. Then there was Elmer's Glue. A little dab of glue was never enough. It had to be a big glob even though you were only gluing a tiny button to the paper. Or, just maybe, you loved Play-Doh.

The World of Play-Doh

Who could ever forget Play-Doh? Bright yellow cans, a soft compound, and the unforgettable smell. More than two billion cans of Play-Doh, weighing more than 700 million pounds, have been sold since it first hit store shelves in 1956. That's enough Play-Doh to make a "snake" with the Fun Factory® that would wrap around the world nearly 300 times.[19]

Play-Doh was originally available in one brilliant color—off-white. Today you can get Play-Doh in a wide assortment of colors like Rose Red, Purple Paradise, Blue Lagoon, or Garden Green. And for those hard-core Play-Doh fanatics, there's even wood-scented Play-Doh for use with your Play-Doh Power Drill Kit or Buzzin' Buzz Saw.[20] Add to that the fast-food Play-Doh gadgets and the Doh-Ville Fuzzy-Farm Animals, and you have the makings of a kid's Play-Doh Dream World.

Thinking is Like Play-Doh

Thinking is a lot like Play-Doh—it can be soft and pliable or it can stink, get dry, hard and crumbly, and become completely useless. I see "useless" thinking more than ever in organizations steeped in bureaucratic red tape, and churches more committed to their traditions than reaching people far from God. Too often, people in these environments come to the table with fresh ideas only to be scorched by the hot, dry sun of archaic thinking.

As dangerous as that is on an organizational level, it is equally dangerous on a personal level. When our Growth TRAC leads us to new discoveries, how we respond mentally is the ultimate test. We can allow our new discoveries to replace stale and irrelevant thinking, or we can hold on to dry, crumbling thinking that's as useless as Play-Doh baked under the desert sun.

Unfortunately, many people never realize their full missional potential because they don't move beyond the Learning Level to a place where their thinking is stretched. They operate like robots conformed to systems, methods, and traditions, while never exploring the possibilities that lie just beyond their self-imposed prison.

Such thinking is disastrous and usually precedes missed opportunities, stifled growth, and a shift out of step with God. This kind of thinking is why once successful businesses shut down after years of operation. It's why organizations plateau after a vibrant launch. It's why churches lose their influence on culture. It's why many followers of Christ, steeped in rules and regulations, experience distance in their relationship with God. Jesus himself recognized such thinking among the Pharisees and teachers of the law when He said, "You nullify the word of God for the sake of your tradition."[21] The way you think affects everything.

Rigid thinking is not an age thing. I've met people who are young, yet practice outdated and ineffective thinking. I've also met people well beyond retirement who demonstrate extremely fresh thinking—the result of a lifelong commitment to personal growth. Thinking is not an *age* thing but rather a *growth* thing. The longer you grow, the longer your thinking remains fresh. Unfortunately, while most people physically work into their sixties, many mentally retire shortly after they graduate school. That's why the Thinking Level of personal growth is so crucial. Without it, you accumulate information without changing your thought patterns...much less your life.

Characteristics of the Thinking Level

Physicist and Nobel Prize winner Albert Einstein once observed, "Thinking is hard work; that's why so few do it." It's amazing how easy it is to learn without ever changing your thinking. Some would argue that such learning isn't possible, insisting that true learning only happens

"Thinking is hard work; that's why so few do it."

when your behavior changes. But haven't we all seen people quote Scripture, recite facts, or pass an exam without changing how they think, much less how they behave? They learned the facts and acquired the knowledge for the sake of short-term gains while their thinking remained fastened to the magnet of yesterday's thought patterns.

To maximize personal growth, the giant magnet keeping you confined to the junkyard of poor thinking must be demagnetized. That process takes place at the Thinking Level of personal growth. You'll know you've reached the Thinking Level when three dominant characteristics are evident. First, a growth attitude develops. Second, beliefs and assumptions are challenged and formed. And third, life is viewed through the lens of what you've learned. Let's explore each of these in more detail.

A GROWTH ATTITUDE DEVELOPS

While a person with a healthy learning posture is knowledge-able, more than anything they acknowledge how much they *don't* know. When you're in this situation, you're usually at or beyond the Thinking Level of personal growth. Why? Because you've developed the right attitude about growth.

Your attitude is like the culture of your mind. The culture of a country defines how the people think and live...it's the "normal" that exists in that country. What's normal for one country may be abnormal for another because every country has its own way of doing things. Your mind has a "normal" too—a culture of sorts—that is comprised of your attitudes. Your normal may be different from my normal, but in both cases, our attitudes shape our normal. And ultimately, those attitudes shape the outlook and outcomes of our lives.

At the Thinking Level, a powerful attitude is formed—a new culture if you will—that is bent toward growth. This attitude of growth, or mental growth culture, yearns for a continual influx of knowledge. Your hunger for personal growth picks up speed because you no longer view growth as an optional add-on feature. Now you see it as the electrical system that brings power to every area of your life. **At the Thinking Level, growing**

moves from a neat idea to a necessary attitude. It becomes part of who you are. It defines your new normal.

UCLA basketball coaching legend John Wooden captured the concept of a growth attitude best when he said, "It's what you learn after you know it all that counts." That is the great separator between ideas and attitude. People who "know it all" have ideas that work now. But people who are lifelong learners have attitudes that work for the rest of their lives. They've developed an attitude that embraces the discipline of daily personal growth. And that attitude influences every area of their lives, keeping them relevant.

How would you describe your attitude? Is it bent toward continual growth and improvement? Despite what others might say or the circumstances that surround you, the chisel that shaped your mental culture is in *your* hand, not somebody else's. *You* are the creator of your mind's culture. So if you don't like the culture of your mind—the very way that you think—then something needs to change...quick.

Your Growth TRAC will certainly help because it provides a personal roadmap for change. But to change your attitude is not easy. Statler and Waldorf, the grumpy old men on the Muppets who hate change, may have taken up residence in your mind. You need to serve them an eviction notice and begin filling your head with new voices—voices that eat, sleep, and breathe a value for personal growth.

When you continually rub shoulders with growing people, their growth attitudes will begin to rub off on you. To develop an attitude of growth, spend more time with "growing friends" and less time with people whose thinking smells like a stale, scum-filled pond. As a wise man once said, "The teaching of the wise is a fountain of life, so, no more drinking from death-tainted wells."[22] Hang out with wise people. When you do, you'll quickly find yourself developing more than growth goals...you'll start developing a growth attitude. And growth attitudes are essential to a personal growth revolution.

BELIEFS AND ASSUMPTIONS ARE CHALLENGED AND FORMED

At the Thinking Level, personal beliefs and assumptions are challenged. This second characteristic of the Thinking Level feels disturbing and uncomfortable because you come face to face with ideas that contradict your long-held traditions. Sometimes this is a breath of fresh air as you gain new insight into a subject or strategy. Other times you won't learn something new, but you'll gain fresh perspective on an old idea. Still other times, your core values and beliefs are challenged and you have to come to grips with *why* you believe what you believe.

This characteristic of the Thinking Level can sound both exciting and scary at the same time—that's because it is. It's exciting because old paradigms are replaced by life-giving thinking. And it's scary because you're forced to wrestle with your most deeply-rooted beliefs. Critical thinking takes place at this level, but you're better for it.

The formation of beliefs and assumptions is a lot like a seesaw—you might have called it a teeter-totter as a kid. When you and your buddy sat on a teeter-totter, you would soar into the air as your feet launched you upward, and then, just as quickly, sink downward as your friend's feet left the ground. While the up and down motion felt exhilarating, and perhaps even unsettling at times, your confidence was grounded in one thing—the base at the center of the seesaw. No matter how quickly you pushed up and how hard you came down, you knew the base wasn't going anywhere. It was your anchor.

At the Thinking Level, a mental teeter-totter is at work. On one end of the seesaw are *ideas*, on the other end are *practices*, and in the middle—serving as the base—are *absolutes*.

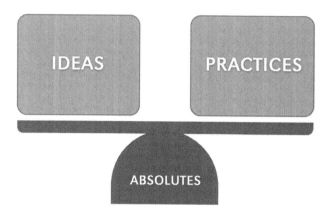

Ideas are insights for living. They can fill your mind rapidly as you read great books, hear inspiring speeches, explore creative environments, or interact with wise mentors. The ideas that emerge from these learning interactions give you fresh insight on how to live life better, how to draw closer to God, how to accelerate your performance at work, how to refine your skills, how to enhance your relationships, or how to improve your health. As you activate your Growth TRAC, there's a good chance your mind will be saturated by fresh ideas in the areas of your life where you've chosen to grow. Some of these ideas will be proven, but others will be more like theories waiting to be tested as a practice.

Practices are strategies for achieving. If you've been around business for any length of time, you've probably heard the phrase, "best practices." Best practices are those methods of doing business that are considered to deliver the best results.

They are usually proven strategies for achieving the highest levels of success. There are also "best practices" in other areas of life too—spiritually, mentally, relationally and physically. And as you engage the Learning Level, you'll likely uncover some of these best practices in the areas where you've chosen to grow.

Ideas and practices freely move up and down on each side of the thinking seesaw. Your mental feet leave the ground as you learn new ideas and experiment with new practices. This flexibility keeps false assumptions and misinformed beliefs from becoming entrenched in your thinking. Eventually you're able to settle on ideas and practices that actually work and leverage them to help you close your growth gaps.

I was working with a team of leaders a while back when we decided to evaluate the effectiveness of our small group ministry. We spent six weeks meeting together to take a hard look at our strengths and weaknesses, as well as ways to improve. This process allowed us to bring our ministry assumptions under the microscope. The mental teeter-totter was aggressively moving up and down as we examined fresh ideas and best practices. At first it almost felt like chaos, unsure where things were going to land. The longer we sat on the thinking seesaw, the more exciting ideas we collected—several of which were untested—and the more we observed powerful best practices. But eventually we settled on a handful of ideas and practices— a refined model—that increased the health of our small groups. None of that would have been possible had we not been willing to challenge our assumptions and get comfortable with letting our feet leave the ground.

Are there areas of your life where you've abandoned the seesaw? Why not get on the teeter-totter once again as you put your Growth TRAC to work. After all, what's the point of crafting a Growth TRAC if you're not willing to challenge your long-held assumptions? Don't be scared of the up and down motion—it's necessary, even indispensable, if you want to gravitate toward the ideas and practices that will actually help you grow. This process is unsettling at times, which is why you need the security of your seesaw's base—*absolutes.*

While ideas and practices are key components to challenging assumptions and forming beliefs, it's important to remember that they are not absolutes. **Absolutes are anchors of belief.** Absolutes are the base of the seesaw. They are fixed—immovable. Absolutes are non-negotiable truth that does not change regardless of time, culture, or geography. In fact, absolute truth originates outside of yourself. Whether or not you believe absolutes does not change the fact that they're still true. Absolutes don't need your or my permission to be the truth—they stand as truth just fine regardless of our opinion. Absolutes are fully trustworthy and apply to everybody. They serve as the litmus test before embracing new beliefs, engaging new practices, or deeming a new idea as worthy of pursuit.

As human beings, we tend to drift toward the path of least resistance. If we're not careful, we'll adopt ideas and practices that are culturally acceptable, yet violate absolute truth. As you field-test ideas and practices, absolute truth keeps you grounded and helps you avoid the dangerous lure of deception. For this reason, I've adopted Original Truth—the Bible—as my source for absolute truth. It is my immovable base. Figure 2 explains why the Bible is qualified to fill this important role.

Figure 2
Defining Your Absolutes

The Bible has withstood the test of time, outlasted those bent on destroying it, and transformed hearts throughout the generations. In their book, *The Faith: Given Once, For All*, Charles Colson and Harold Fickett defend the textual integrity of the Bible, noting that 24,947 ancient manuscripts of the New Testament alone have been discovered, the oldest dating back to AD 150. Scholars have more ancient manuscripts to work from than with any other writing—14,000 of the Old Testament alone. Homer's *Iliad* is the next closest with only 600. And the accuracy of the ancient manuscripts comprising the Scriptures is remarkable. Why? "Jewish tradition provides one answer. According to Hebrew practice, only eyewitness testimony was accepted; and when copying documents, the Jews would copy one letter at a time—not word by word, not phrase by phrase, not sentence by sentence."[23] Although the Bible consists of sixty-six books written over 1,500 years by forty people in three different languages, the story of Scripture provides amazing harmony.

The evidence supporting the authority of the Bible is extraordinary. Colson and Fickett write: "Before the end of the 1950s, no less than 25,000 biblical sites had been substantiated by archaeological discoveries; there has been no discovery proving the Bible false. No other religious document now or in history has ever been found that accurate."[24]

Nevertheless, the Bible has been fought relentlessly. John Wycliffe was an Oxford professor, theologian, and creator of the first hand-written English language Bible manuscripts. Forty-four years after his death on December 31, 1384, Pope Martin V, infuriated by Wycliffe's teachings, ordered his bones to be dug up, crushed, and scattered in the river Swift. In 1415, one of Wycliffe's devout followers, John Hus, was burned at the stake using Wycliffe's manuscript Bibles as kindling for the fire.[25] Despite these, and countless other attempts to destroy the Scriptures, today the publication and distribution of the Bible is available in over 2,000 languages. It is the ultimate authoritative trump card for erroneous beliefs and false assumptions.

What is the base, the immovable absolutes, of *your* thinking seesaw? Without a rock-solid base, your ideas (those insights for living) and your practices (those strategies for achieving) will do more than keep you culturally relevant, they will ever so slowly mislead you. Here are a few questions to help you think about your base:

- What "truth," originating outside of myself, is a credible source to build my life and thinking on?
- Is this "truth" absolute or is it being altered by time, culture, and geography, changing from one generation and from one place to the next?
- Does this "truth" have the power to change the human heart—meaning it's more than rules and regulations and actually has transformational power?

- Who did this "truth" originate with? God or man?

When absolutes are firmly established as the base for your thinking, you can easily challenge your assumptions and beliefs. You can bring the ideas and practices—those things you're gleaning at the Learning Level—into the light where you can examine their validity. And you can climb onto the thinking seesaw—grounded in absolute truth—where you can continually explore fresh ideas and best practices.

Embracing absolutes does not mean you'll live a sinless life. I believe Scripture is absolute truth, but I struggle every day to *live* that truth. I'm far from perfect. I sin. It's a daily battle. But having a firm base to anchor my life and thinking to keeps me calibrated in the right direction. Without the base, my life would be nothing more than a soupy mess of misguided philosophies. Even the Apostle Paul said, "See to it that no one takes you captive through hollow and deceptive philosophy, which depends on human tradition and the basic principles of this world rather than on Christ" (Colossians 2:8).

At the Thinking Level of personal growth, beliefs are challenged and formed by learning new *ideas* and embracing best *practices* while allowing *absolutes* to serve as the final authority. Keep these three things in perspective.

Don't concede an absolute for the sake of an idea or practice—doing so is a compromise of *integrity.* People have diametrically-opposed opinions about what is good, right, or true, which in itself reveals a core flaw—two opposites cannot both be true. Therefore, truth does not start with man, but with God. He is the originator of truth. To concede these absolutes in exchange for my ideas or practices is to relinquish the wholeness and completeness that comes with true integrity. The only thing worse than *not* growing is growing in the *wrong direction.* When you violate absolutes for the sake of a preference or personal opinion, your growth is leading you in the wrong direction.

At the same time, you cannot turn an idea or practice into an absolute—doing so is a compromise of *innovation.* In other words, when you turn something into an absolute truth—such as a preference, tradition, or personal opinion—you become irrelevant. Activist, filmmaker, and innovator Erwin McManus says, "When we evaluate our methodologies or practices, we tend to see them in the context of good and evil. We know to stop doing those things that are wrong and to continue doing those things that are right, but rarely do we evaluate between the good and the best."[26]

Choosing the best might violate tradition but that does not mean you've aligned yourself with evil. Best practices and authoritative truth can peacefully coexist. Integrity and innovation work beautifully together when you embrace great ideas with best practices without sacrificing absolute truth. When you use this filter to challenge your beliefs and assumptions, your thinking remains fresh, solid, and fruitful.

> *Integrity and innovation work beautifully together when you embrace great ideas with best practices without sacrificing absolute truth.*

LIFE IS VIEWED THROUGH THE LENS OF WHAT YOU'VE LEARNED

My wife and I enjoy watching movies. We love an engaging storyline. Although we typically watch the same films, we do so through a different set of lenses. Karen loves history, counseling, and fashion, so when she watches a movie, she's quickly attuned to historical accuracy, the needs of the characters, the décor of the set, and the clothes worn by each actor. Why? Because she has a degree in history, a Master's in counseling, a love for nice clothes, and an eye for beautiful décor. Her learning in these areas has shaped the lens through which she watches movies.

I'm completely different. It doesn't even occur to me, unless it's completely obvious, that the historical timeline of the movie may be inaccurate. And I don't care what the actors wear, as long as they have on clothes. For me, I watch movies through a different lens—the leadership lens. My antenna is always up, looking for the leadership lesson in every film I watch. Sometimes it's a very strong leadership lesson, other times very subtle. I watch movies from this perspective because I've spent years reading, studying, developing, and practicing leadership. It's what I'm passionate about. And because I've spent a considerable amount of time learning leadership, it shapes the lens through which I view life. This might sound like a mental workout routine when you're simply trying to relax and enjoy a movie. But it's really not. It just comes naturally...it's who I've become.

You're the same way—you view life through a unique lens. You notice something different when you watch a movie—that *something* is almost always defined by the areas where you've learned the most and grown the most. So as you grow, you'll know you've moved to the Thinking Level when you begin to view life through the filter of what you gleaned at the Learning Level.

This doesn't mean you've wiped out everything else from your mind and focused solely on what you recently learned. It simply means that you're letting the things you've learned shape your perspective on life. For example, if you recently learned something that's relevant to a conversation you're having at work, then what you learned should shape how you think about that conversation...and ultimately the words that come out of your mouth. Otherwise, you haven't moved to the Thinking Level.

Play-Doh Revisited

So how do you know when you've reached the Thinking Level? Three characteristics are evident in your life: you've developed a growth attitude, your beliefs and assumptions are being challenged and formed, and you're beginning to view life through the filter of what you have learned. These are important distinctions because they usually requires a higher level of consistency in learning to remove dry, crumbly thinking and replace it with fresh insight.

It's like Play-Doh that's become a bit too dry. I once read the instructions on the side of a Play-Doh can. They said, "If necessary, water may be added one drop at a time to restore softness." Your mind needs repeated drops of personal growth—found in your Growth TRAC—to cultivate the mental pliability needed for good thinking. And with each drop, the characteristics of the Thinking Level are formed in your life. As we will discover in the next chapter, there's a single practice at the Thinking Level that brings these characteristics to life. When that practice is embraced, your personal growth revolution exhibits truly mature thinking.

Chapter 6 ---

Reflective Thinking: All Grown Up

History is filled with stories of men and women who inspired great change to create a better world for others who didn't have a voice. One such man was William Wilberforce, the slave abolitionist who literally altered the course of mankind's thinking. In the late 1700s, English traders were routinely raiding the African coast, capturing thousands of Africans each year, shipping them across the Atlantic, and selling them into slavery. This horrible practice continued to escalate until slavery was firmly entrenched in British culture. In fact, slavery was so common that it was not only considered perfectly acceptable, but it was actually viewed as an essential component for the empire's economic stability. Without the benefit of slave labor, British industry simply could not remain competitive in the world.

In 1780, at only 21 years of age, Wilberforce was elected to England's Parliament. Although he was a gifted social climber, his personal ambitions were frivolous in the beginning. Later in his life he would write, "The first years in Parliament

I did nothing—nothing to any purpose. My own distinction was my darling object."[27] At that time, accustomed to a life of privilege, Wilberforce thought quite a lot of himself. Like most everyone else in Parliament, he was content with a luxurious lifestyle, leveraging his power as just another means of personal gain.

It wasn't until 1784, after having spent some time with an Anglican clergyman, Isaac Milner, that Wilberforce began to reconsider his life's ambition. As they studied the Greek New Testament together, Wilberforce grew more and more convinced of his own need for God's mercy. By October of 1785, after seeking counsel from John Newton, an Anglican evangelical living in London, Wilberforce fully embraced a faith in Christ.

Immediately following this experience—which he would refer to for the rest of his life as his "great change"—Wilberforce considered leaving politics to pursue ministry as his full-time vocation. Disgusted with himself and his youthful, selfish political ambitions, he felt trading his past for a life in the clergy was a reasonable next step following his conversion. However, John Newton, along with Wilberforce's close friend, William Pitt, had a much grander vision of what it meant to be on mission with God. They challenged Wilberforce to climb down from the traditional pulpit he was favoring and to instead acknowledge Parliament as his ministry.

Wilberforce was torn. His ambitions had changed. He was no longer infatuated by political games or vain socializing. He carved out very intentional spaces in his busy schedule to be alone to *pray, question,* and *reflect* on God's next step for him. He clearly understood the massive weight of the decision he was considering, realizing that no matter what he concluded, it would change the very course of his life. He was determined to choose wisely.

Wilberforce finally arrived at his verdict. He wrote in his diary, "My walk is a public one. My business is in the world, and I must mix in the assemblies of men or quit the post which Providence seems to have assigned me."[28] Of course, he intended that this time things would be different. Wilberforce exchanged his earlier superficial ambitions for a new aim, a noble purpose. Instead of using his influence to build a self-serving résumé, he dedicated his life to two great causes: the restoration of morals in British society, and the abolition of slavery.

Although Wilberforce's decision to fight slavery was extremely unpopular, particularly among the aristocracy and wealthy who had always been his friends, his Christian worldview[29] left him no choice. Wilberforce refused to simply learn *about* truth while simultaneously conveniently ignoring the atrocities of slavery.

Instead, he *reflected* on the things he learned, emerging from his quiet times with conviction-filled beliefs. Then he leveraged his newfound beliefs—primarily his repulsion at the evils of slavery—to continually motivate himself to inspire change. He wrote, "So enormous, so dreadful, so irremediable did the trade's wickedness appear that my own mind was completely made up for abolition. Let the consequences be what they would: I from this time determined that I would never rest until I had effected its abolition."[30]

Ending slavery in Britain wasn't going to happen overnight. The journey was long, difficult, and painful. Over the course of years, Wilberforce introduced numerous resolutions and bills against the slave trade, finding himself turned back again and again. His opponents slandered him, attacked his character and motives, used his past against him, and even threatened him. His anguish, coupled with nonstop work, repeatedly weakened him, pushing him into long bouts against illness. But Wilberforce persevered. It took 18 long years. On March 25, 1807, the Abolition of the Slave Trade bill finally received Royal Assent. Although the bill provided that it would still be legal to own existing slaves, the industry of capturing and trading slaves was outlawed once and for all.

In the years that followed, Wilberforce relentlessly labored to ensure that the new slave trade laws were enforced. He worked tirelessly, educating slaves to prepare them for their freedom. On July 26, 1833, the House of Commons passed the Slavery Abolition Act. Three days later, William Wilberforce died. And less than one month later, the House of Lords passed the act. All slaves living in the British Empire were finally freed.

GO! Practice #2: Reflective Thinking: How to Move to the Thinking Level

Where did Wilberforce win the battle to abolish slavery? While his fight was long and difficult, his first real victory took place inside his own mind. Wilberforce cultivated a deliberate practice—a filter of sorts—for his thoughts. He embraced *reflective thinking*—the Go! Practice of the Thinking Level of personal growth. **Reflective thinking is the habit of processing what you've learned in preparation for personal application.** This practice helped Wilberforce apply his Christian worldview to the most pressing needs of his time. It helped him think carefully about what he gleaned at the Learning Level and gave him the perspective to reach his missional potential. To employ reflective thinking requires three things: *time, questions,* and *takeaways*.

TIME

Reflective thinking is, for the most part, very unnatural—especially for high-achievers and dominant personality types. These individuals are "doers," so they rarely feel they have a minute to spare. This means that they often view setting aside *think time* as a *waste of time.*

If our personality bent and "need to achieve" isn't enough, all of us feel the pressure to live life at a breakneck pace. The tyranny of the urgent has moved in to the spare bedroom of our minds, mooching off of us like an unwanted deadbeat relative who can't hold down a job. And when the tyranny to get more done overrides your need for reflective thinking, what happens to your personal growth? If you're like most people, just trying to keep your head above water, you probably put it on a shelf labeled "Someday I'll...":

- "Someday I'll spend more time with God, but right now school is consuming me."
- "Someday I'll invest more time with my kids, but right now I just don't have the energy."
- "Someday I'll be more intentional about my growth, but right now work is killin' me."
- "Someday I'll get in shape, but even if I wanted to do that now, I just don't have the time to work out consistently."

It's so easy to let "Someday I'll..." become your personal growth default button. And for a while, you won't feel any consequences.

But what happens during these times? Where do our minds wander as the rat race accelerates? What kind of thinking patterns do we naturally gravitate toward? Slowly, predictably, almost without realizing it, our thinking will return to our well-worn safety nets of false assumptions and misguided beliefs, as if they'll be able to save us. Old thinking habits die hard. Glen Beaman once said, "Stubbornness does have its helpful features. You always know what you're going to be thinking tomorrow." If that sounds pretty good to you, take it as a warning sign. When your personal growth pool dries up, you'll have nothing new to reflect on. When you cash your personal growth in to pay your urgency taxes, your thinking heads straight to the bankrupt account of outdated practices and tired strategies.

Reflective thinking takes time, which means you have to intentionally cut things out of your schedule to make room for this practice. Don't think you have anywhere to make cuts? How many hours do you spend randomly surfing the net? How many times do you have to work late hours because you didn't manage your "9 to 5" window wisely? Or how many hours do you spend each week glued to your TV? According to one Nielsen report, the average American watches 153 hours of television per month.[31] That's over 6 days per month, 76 days per year, and more than 14 years in a lifetime! I'm not asking you to completely cut entertainment from your life. But put things in perspective. Scale back in one area to make room to reflect.

I often take time for reflective thinking after reading a couple of chapters in a book. This valuable time helps me process what I've just read against the backdrop of my current life circumstances. Reflective thinking allows me both to absorb the words and to ponder their call to action. These reflection breaks are like the gaps between meals—they give me a chance to digest what I've been learning.

What about you? When was the last time you spent 30 minutes reflecting? I'm not suggesting that you stand staring out your bedroom window, scratching your head, wondering what in the world you're going to think about. What I'm suggesting is that you work the system of your Growth TRAC and intentionally set aside time to reflect on the things that you're learning. Your goal is not simply to acquire more information; you need to filter the good from the bad so you can apply what's *best* to your daily life. Reflective thinking makes that possible.

QUESTIONS

Socrates said, "The unexamined life is not worth living." The greatest tool for examination is questions. Wilberforce spent a lot of time asking questions. He didn't rush his process of reflective thinking. He carefully considered the impact of his faith not only on his own future, but on England's future as well.

Organizational consultants Dan Sullivan and Catherine Nomura wisely counsel, "Always make your questions bigger than your answers, and you'll keep drawing yourself into a bigger future with new possibilities."[32] Asking questions opens spiritual, mental, relational, and physical doors of growth. Questions allow you to see glimpses into a bigger future in the most important areas of your life. The key is to ask the *right* questions. As you follow your roadmap—those clear action steps in each of your Growth TRACs—be sure to ask yourself these six reflection questions:

1. Mission
   How can what I'm learning close my growth gaps and help me fulfill my life's mission?

2. Beliefs
   How does what I'm learning change or reinforce my core beliefs? Does any of what I'm learning violate absolute truth?

3. Assumptions
   How is my learning challenging attitudes and assumptions I have about my roles, circumstances, and paradigms?

4. Character
   How can what I'm learning shape my character?

5. Methods
   Is what I'm learning a better strategy, practice, or technique for attaining superior results in my roles and responsibilities?

6. Relationships
   How can what I'm learning improve my relationships?

These are tough questions to answer. But if you'll take the time to ask them of yourself, your answers can provide the breakthroughs you need to grow to the next level.

Sometimes I'll set aggressive goals in my job. When I do, I always seem to come to the same realization: To achieve the new goals I've set, I'm going to have to change how I think. You face the same dilemma. Everybody does. In fact, our number one problem at work—or for that matter, in any area of our lives—is not lack. It's not a lack of time, a lack of talent, or even a lack of money. *It's falling short in how we think.* Our thinking deficit creates time, talent, and money deficits. As Albert Einstein once observed, "You cannot achieve a new goal by apply-

ing the same level of thinking that got you where you are today."
And yet how many times do we try
to do just that?

> "You cannot achieve a new goal by applying the same level of thinking that got you where you are today."

You have to challenge your thinking by asking questions. You must leave the shores of routine thinking and set sail for a new horizon—one where your questions lead you to a land of new growth. Unless you're willing to ask and answer the mind-stretching questions, you'll live confined to the world as you currently know it. Ask the questions...and then have the guts to answer them honestly. Then, when your answers reveal a difficult reality, don't pretend you never saw it. Use the questions as fuel for your growth.

TAKEAWAYS

When you take time to reflect, and when you're willing to answer the tough questions, takeaways will naturally emerge. Just like mining, you have to survey, dig, and sift to get the gold out of what you're learning. "But hasn't my Growth TRAC pinpointed what I'm going to learn?" Yes and no. Your Growth TRAC determines what you'll learn and in which areas of your life you plan to grow. Remember, it's your track to run on. But reflective thinking makes your learning *relevant* to you. That's what makes the Thinking Level distinct.

As you wrestle with paradigms, assumptions, and beliefs, the adjustments you make in your thinking—or for that matter, the ones you don't make—will determine whether your learning has any long-term impact on your life. As I said before, your goal isn't just to acquire more information. Your goal is to change your life. Just as with cramming for a test, you can "learn" without growing. But you can't effect long-term change through shortcuts. Your Growth TRAC sets the path for your learning, but reflective thinking helps you make that learning personal, applicable, and meaningful. Technically, you could have the exact same Growth TRAC as somebody else (which I don't necessarily recommend), yet you would likely observe completely different outcomes. The Thinking Level allows you to *filter* what you're learning through the unique lens of your life and circumstances.

> *Your Growth TRAC sets the path for your learning, but reflective thinking helps you make that learning personal, applicable, and meaningful.*

When William Wilberforce took the time for reflective thinking, it culminated in crucial, life-altering takeaways. Those takeaways informed his decisions about how to invest his time, resources, and influence. For example, Wilberforce pursued numerous philanthropic causes—69 at one time, in fact. His friends and observers dubbed him "the prime minister of a cabinet of philanthropists." He gave one-fourth of his annual income to the poor. He fought on behalf of chimney sweeps, single mothers, Sunday schools, orphans, and juvenile delinquents. He helped start the Society for Bettering the Cause of the Poor, the Church Missionary Society, the British Foreign Bible Society, and the Antislavery Society.[33] None of this would have happened if he had neglected reflective thinking. It was this practice that clarified his worldview and settled his core convictions, ultimately determining how he would impact society.

Let's make takeaways personal to you. This is the sixth chapter of this book. There's a good chance you've picked up a few insights or learned some helpful ideas getting here. There's also a good chance that you'll forget many (most) of these insights and ideas if you don't take the time to reflect on them. Don't beat yourself up over it—focusing on the short-term is human nature. We all do it.

Stop right now, block out some time (say 30 minutes). Take out a sheet of paper. Flip back and scan through the first few chapters and ask yourself, "What are the biggest takeaways I've gotten from each chapter so far?" Each time you come across a take-away, something meaningful to you that you want to remember and perhaps use later, jot it down in your own words. Don't necessarily try for complete sentences. Stick to key words and phrases. Just be sure you capture enough that you'll later be able to pull up what was meaningful. (It may even be a good idea to write the page number next to each takeaway where that idea came to you.)

Once you're caught up with where we are in chapter six, don't stop. Continue writing down takeaways as you encounter them throughout the rest of the book. At any point when you decide you're ready to effect some changes in your life, review your list, reflect on each item, and choose 3–5 takeaways that you want to apply to your life. In the next couple of chapters, we'll talk specifics about how to apply what you're learning.

From Reflective Thinking to Mental Maturity

Reflective Thinking is the GO! PRACTICE of the Thinking Level of personal growth. Reflective thinking will help you filter, process, adopt best practices, assimilate meaningful ideas, affirm truths, and dismantle your false beliefs and assumptions. *The OUTCOME of this practice is Mental Maturity.* Romans 12:2 gives us a snapshot of what this process looks like: "Do not conform any longer to the pattern of this world, but be transformed by the renewing of your mind. Then you will be able to test and approve what God's will is—his good, pleasing and perfect will." The Message really brings home the essence of the Thinking Level:

> Don't become so well-adjusted to your culture that you fit into it without even thinking. Instead, fix your attention on God. You'll be changed from the inside out. Readily recognize what he wants from you, and quickly respond to it. Unlike the culture around you, always dragging you down to its level of immaturity, God brings the best out of you, *develops well-formed maturity in you*."[34]

Reflective thinking is the practice that leads you to mental maturity. It helps you sort through the onslaught of ideas, emerging with mature thoughts, ideas, practices, beliefs, and a biblically sound worldview.

Maybe the idea of reflective thinking doesn't appeal to you. Maybe it sounds boring, or too slow, or like too much work and effort. If you find yourself struggling with reflective thinking, look once again at your personality type (Appendix B) for clues on how to address that. If you thrive in relational settings, don't try to reflect alone. Invite a friend to coffee, take your list, and ask them to help you process it. Maybe invite a small group of friends over. Feed them dinner, bring out your list, and get their feedback. Either way, you'll get the chance to think out loud and bounce your thoughts and ideas off of others.

One word of caution: If you have an "adaptable" personality, easily swayed by friends and the opinions of others, carefully consider who you should invite into your reflection process. More than once, I've seen people shipwreck their faith because they lacked the biblical and moral foundation they needed to process difficult issues, especially when they invited others to start challenging their core values and personal beliefs. Be sure the base of your seesaw is sound, and that you know not only what you believe, but why.

Here's what I'm *not* saying: I'm *not* suggesting you should lock yourself in a bubble where everyone else thinks and acts like you. You can't grow without fresh thinking, much of which comes from people who think differently than you do. What I *am* saying: be wise. Really think about who you're going to invite into your reflective thinking circle. This is a critical, important process. Get the best players that you can involved. The Bible says, "Plans fail for lack of counsel, but with many advisors they succeed."[35] Wilberforce surrounded himself with advisors like Isaac Milner, William Pitt, and John Newton, men who helped him think clearly about his faith and about his influence on culture. Choose your advisors carefully.

Avoiding the "Thinking" Ditch

The most likely place we'll stumble will be in our thinking. Too often we try to produce new growth revolutions using the same thinking that got us to where we are now. That simply doesn't work. How we think—and the fact that we often don't—is the prophet of our future. Too many people want the payoff without paying the price for personal growth. They have an attitude of minimal gains that throws their personal growth into the ditch.

Author and Pastor Andy Stanley offers some insightful advice for emerging generations who are facing this temptation:

> *"In the early years of your career, what you learn is far more important than what you earn. In most cases, what you learn early on will determine what you earn later on."*[36]

"In the early years of your career, what you learn is far more important than what you earn. In most cases, what you learn early on will determine what you earn later on." I sure wish I had heard this earlier in my life. This is exactly what I *didn't* do in the early days of my career. There were probably people trying to tell me this, but I just didn't listen to them in high school (or in college either, for that matter). In fact, I didn't go to school to learn...I went to graduate. You may think, "That doesn't make sense. Don't you have to learn *something* to get to graduate?" Well, that depends on which school you went to (but that's another story).

Seriously, my goal was simply to finish school so that *then* I could do the things I really wanted to. Little did I know at the time, I was undermining my potential with an immature attitude of pursuing minimal gains. My thinking was messed up. If I happened to grow enough that it opened a door of opportunity, I didn't feel I had to keep growing to *keep* that door open. But the truth is that what gets you where you are won't keep you there—and it certainly won't get you where you want to go. You can't apply minimal effort to your personal growth and expect your life to change. That's like trying to start a communications company without staying up-to-date with emerging technologies; eventually everything you know will be obsolete, and you'll have to hang an "out of business" sign—on your mind.

You also can't rely on popular thinking to shape your mind. As Kevin Myers once said, "The problem with popular thinking is that it doesn't require you to think at all." Rather than challenging "common knowledge," we often adopt it as our own. We feel accepted because we think we're just like everybody else. So our "please the crowd" immaturity thrives as our mental maturity evaporates. As you follow your Growth TRAC, you'll likely learn new ideas and best practices, but the Thinking Level requires you to carefully reflect on them before assimilating these new insights into your life.

If what you gleaned at the Learning Level isn't shaping your thinking, and you find yourself being pulled toward popular thinking or an attitude of minimal gains, take a good look at that ditch on the side of the road...the one with your name on it. You'll have lots of company in that ditch. It's filled with men and women who once dreamed great dreams but slowly grew content, even comfortable, with an "easy" life of meager growth. And even though that ditch looks full, there's always room for one more procrastinating mind. Let the ditch—that desolate crater of wasted potential—motivate you to get your thinking realigned. Don't settle for minimal gains. Don't chase popular thinking. Avoid the "thinking" ditch by feeding your appetite for lifelong learning and reflecting on the insights you've learned.

The Thinking Level of personal growth is a powerful processing point in your growth journey. Using the GO! Practice of *reflective thinking*, you'll be able to carefully and wisely filter what you're learning and cultivate Christ-honoring *mental maturity*. As this happens, you'll feel your growth revolution churning inside, like a hive of fresh ideas and insights buzzing with excitement, just looking for a place to be used in the real world. When that happens, you're standing at the threshold of the third level of personal growth—*Living.*

GO! Starting a Personal Growth Revolution				
GO! Practice	Activates	Level of Personal Growth	Which results in	Outcome
Growth TRACing	⟶	The Learning Level	⟶	Growth Traction
Reflective Thinking	⟶	The Thinking Level	⟶	Mental Maturity

Chapter 7

The Living Level: Your Personal Growth Hinge

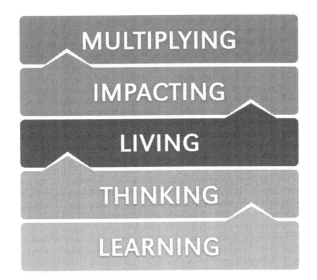

On December 17, 1903, two bicycle builders from Dayton, Ohio, changed the definition of the word "impossible." At 10:35 on a cold, windy morning, the *Wright Flyer* made its maiden voyage—a mere 120 feet in 12 seconds—four miles south of Kitty Hawk, North Carolina. This singular feat was the culminating tour-de-force of years of Wilbur and Orville Wright's deliberate and focused work. More notably, it was the crown jewel of the Wright brothers' commitment to personal growth.

Wilbur had already been moderately interested in flying, but it took reading in 1896 about the death of Otto Lilienthal, an early aviation pioneer, to finally shake his curiosity fully awake. Although the glider accident that claimed Lilienthal's life was a definite setback in the quest for manned flight, that event planted a seed in both of the Wrights that would grow and grow, constantly nourished by the research they were devoting to the subject of flight.

Personal growth practices weren't new to either of them. Wilbur, especially, was an avid reader, often spending hours a day devouring literature, history, or theology. And when a hockey accident squelched his aspirations to attend Yale, Wilbur refused to waste a single day of his recovery. For three years he disciplined himself to read and study in his father's library.[37] Neither Wilbur nor Orville ever attended college—the only two in the Wright family not to do so. But that fact didn't squelch the personal growth revolution growing inside of them. Orville later wrote, "We were lucky enough to grow up in an environment where there was always much encouragement to children to pursue intellectual interests; to investigate whatever aroused curiosity."[38]

Growing Toward a Dream

Like an onion, the Wrights peeled back the mystery of aviation, one layer after another. They scrutinized every piece of literature on the subject of flight. Personal growth was not merely a necessity to reach some obscure goal. The Wrights deliberately breathed it in like oxygen, bringing life to their aviation pursuits. Their personal growth didn't stop with the printed page, either. They were obsessive bird watchers. They experimented with the ideas their interests generated, constantly seeking specific answers out of ambiguities.

For three years, they devoured books, making frequent visits to the Dayton Public Library. They wrote to the Smithsonian Institute requesting materials on aviation. They read magazine articles. They engaged in lively debates with one another, comparing notes and concocting wild theories. Finally, Wilbur and Orville emerged from their process with a workable, realistic concept for manned flight. Author and management expert Mark Eppler reports these telling words from a letter Wilbur wrote: "...we soon passed from the reading to the thinking, and finally to the working stage."[39] Less than two years after they had fleshed out their concept, the Wrights' theory became the reality of flight.

Characteristics of the Living Level

Wilbur and Orville Wright's story captures the very essence of the Living Level of personal growth. The Wrights couldn't settle for simply *learning it* and *thinking it.* Eventually they had to *do it.* As Eppler observes, "Knowledge gained but unapplied remains nothing more than potential."[40] I would add: *wasted* potential.

The Living Level of personal growth is all about transformation. It's where you put into practice the knowledge that you first acquired at the Learning Level, then later reflected on at the Thinking Level. The Living Level puts the wheels on the bicycle, the wings on the plane. Without application, the Learning Level and the Thinking Level have no power. Without application, the Impacting Level and the Multiplying Level will have no potential. The Living Level is the hinge on which the other levels swing. At the Living Level you transition purposefully from philosophy to practice, from contemplation to concrete action. It lifts you off the ground of good intentions into the wild blue yonder of execution.

The Bible describes the Living Level in James 1:22: "Do not merely listen to the word, and so deceive yourselves. Do what it says." But James doesn't stop there. He bluntly lays out the truth: "...faith by itself, if it is not accompanied by action, is dead."[41] If James had been writing about the five levels of personal growth, he might have said, **"You've learned something, you've thought about it, DO it...NOW. Don't wait!"**

Three characteristics define the Living Level of personal growth. Each one builds on the one previous to shift your personal behaviors into new, unexplored territory.

1. Reflective Thinking Culminates in Clear Decisions
2. Clear Decisions Lead to New Habits
3. New Habits Demonstrate a Transformed Life

REFLECTIVE THINKING CULMINATES IN CLEAR DECISIONS

The first characteristic of the Living Level is the clarity that results from reflective thinking—clarity about how to *apply* to your life what you've learned. Achieving this point of clarity isn't always easy. In fact, it rarely is. Most of what you need is time. One practical way to speed up the process is to keep a journal or a writing pad, and diligently capture your reflective thoughts.

Writing helps you sort through your thoughts, crystallize your ideas, and queue the strongest candidates onto your runway of decision. On paper, your thoughts are completely safe. A journal is an airplane hangar where you can tinker with your ideas and dream big, looking for which ones might be flight worthy in your life. But eventually, you have to complete your tinkering, or those thoughts can never leave the hangar and taxi down the runway. When your thoughts take flight as decisions, up in the air is where all your clever engineering will either pay off or break up. Once in the air, if your decision falters, both you and its passengers (the people you influence) will find yourselves scrambling for parachutes, as your grand idea spirals out of control. The end may see you cleaning up at your crash site: doing damage control in your own life, even as you face the consequences of how your decision's fiery crash may have impacted the course of others' lives. Experimental flying is dangerous business.

Shaping your thoughts into decisions bridges the Thinking Level across to the Living Level. This process picks up where the Thinking Level ended, carrying your reflective thinking forward

Reflective thinking is all about sorting through your options. Application is all about selecting just one.

toward solid, specific application points. Of course, you can't apply everything you learn. It's humanly impossible. You have to inspect your long menu of options, reflect on each, and then select the one or two that will make the most sense for your life. Reflective thinking is all about sorting through your options. Application is all about selecting just one.

CLEAR DECISIONS LEAD TO NEW HABITS

Your life is the result of your "inside decisions." Inside decisions define your habits—whether good or bad. What happens on the inside manifests itself by your habits on the outside. This is the second characteristic of the Living Level.

In Colossians 1:9, the Apostle Paul writes, "...we have not stopped praying for you and asking God to fill you with the knowledge of his will through all spiritual wisdom and understanding." This verse reveals a natural progression in the growth process: It begins first with knowledge, then moves toward spiritual wisdom and understanding. The word Paul used for knowledge is *epignōsis* (eh-PIG-noh-sis). Author and professor Dr. William Yount describes epignōsis as "a knowledge that reaches out and grasps its object and is in turn grasped by its object." **What you learn becomes more than knowledge—it changes how you live.** You grasp the knowledge, and the knowledge grasps you. It forms a new habit.

Yount further observes, "Epignōsis moves beyond mere head knowledge to what we might call 'heart' knowledge: a knowledge that affects the way we live. To be filled with the *epignōsis* of His will means to take hold of God's Word, and allow God's Word to take hold of us."[42] As this knowledge becomes *understanding*, it finds application—what Jesus calls "wisdom." He says in Matthew 7:24, "Therefore everyone who hears these words of mine and puts them into practice is like a *wise* man who built his house on the rock." *(emphasis mine)*.

> At the Learning level, you gain knowledge. At the Thinking level, you come to understand that knowledge. At the Living level, you finally see it translated into wisdom—through application.

At the Learning level, you gain knowledge. At the Thinking level, you come to understand that knowledge. At the Living level, you finally see it translated into wisdom—through application.

Let's get practical. Pick one thing you've learned since you created your Growth TRAC. It might be something in your spiritual life, or perhaps a relationship, a best practice at work, or a better way to take care of your health. After you acquired this new knowledge, did you take time to reflect on it? If so, what takeaways did you discover? Now, which takeaways do you need to act on? Don't wait. Today, decide to apply at least one of these takeaways to your life. When you do, you'll form new habits and unleash the power of the Living Level.

When you decide to apply what you've been learning, you walk right into new habits. You begin actually doing what you've been learning and thinking about. You leap from possibles to actuals. Remember that debate that raged inside you at the Thinking Level? The Living Level silences it once and for all. The rubber meets the road. You're committed. President John F. Kennedy once said, "There are risks and costs to a program of action. But they are far less than the long-range risks and costs of comfortable inaction." You just passed the last exit for comfortable inaction. The risks of action are straight ahead.

NEW HABITS DEMONSTRATE A TRANSFORMED LIFE

The final characteristic of the Living Level is the evidence of a transformed life. Your heart races. Your eyes sparkle. Genuine progress invigorates you. No more "What if?" Everything's actually happening. You're doing more than accumulating knowledge; now you're applying its lessons to your everyday life. The things you decide aren't just idealistic; they're realistic. You're practicing, implementing, and completely applying. Your knowing has become your growing. At the Living Level, you're not just pointing to how you *want* to grow; now you're pointing to the evidence that you *are* growing. Your learning feeds new habits (habits of the head, hands, and heart), which demonstrate a transformed life.

Personal transformation is difficult. Human beings resist change, and the process of forming new habits isn't easy. And while we work hard to form new habits of the head (how we think) and new habits of the hands (what we do), changing habits of the heart is entirely different. Your heart represents the very core of who you are, which is why it's the hardest thing to change in your life. The best way—in fact, the only way—to reach true, honest, heart transformation at the Living Level is to allow the Spirit of Christ to do the transforming. If you try to just "do" the right behaviors without God's Spirit changing you on the inside, you'll find yourself with little more than two legalistic lists: Do's and Don'ts. Don't do that to yourself. **Your Work (the discipline) x God's Work (the transformation) = Exponential Life Change**

The writer of Hebrews chastised the Hebrew Christians for being "slow to learn." (Hebrews 5:11) He wasn't criticizing their mental abilities. It was their spiritual laziness that was the problem. They were resisting the path to maturity by staying on "milk" instead of moving up to "solid food." Hebrews 5:14 says, "But solid food is for the mature, who by constant use have trained themselves to distinguish good from evil." To get that maturity, you have to fully trust Christ and practice personal application through disciplined intentionality.

Notice that both "constant use" and "training yourself" are required. In fact, Jesus said, "If you just use my words in Bible studies and don't work them into your life, you are like a stupid carpenter who built his house on the sandy beach. When a storm rolled in and the waves came up, it collapsed like a house of cards" (Matthew 7:26–27, MSG). Did you catch that? You have to "work" God's word into your life. New habits don't form by themselves. Learning without applying what you have learned is just plain laziness. **Lazy Learning = Lukewarm Living.**

We must do what *we* can do (the discipline), and let God do what only *He* can do (the transformation). The Apostle Paul described God's transforming work when he challenged the church at Ephesus to abandon their old way of life, inviting them instead to "take on an entirely new way of life—a God-fashioned life, a life renewed from the inside and working itself into your conduct as God accurately reproduces his character in you."[43]

What an amazing picture. Take a moment to imagine what it might look like for God to "reproduce his character in you." No matter how much you have your act together, you'll never be able to take the place of God. Reproducing His character inside of us is God's job, not yours or mine. Our job is simply to trust Him and cooperate with His Spirit.

Can you learn without God? Absolutely. People do it all the time. Can you be transformed without God? I guess it depends on how you define transformed. But I'd say no—not "heart" transformation. You simply cannot change your heart without God. You may be able to change your behavior and develop new habits of the head and of the hands. But you can't change the habits of your heart. Only Christ has the power to truly, genuinely, completely transform your human heart.

If you consider yourself a follower of Christ, but you're not willing to allow Him to transform you, then you're what Craig

Groeschel calls a "Christian atheist": you believe in God, but you live as if He doesn't exist.[44] And if you've never surrendered your heart to Christ, are you willing to take that step? Are you willing to say "yes" to the transforming work of the Holy Spirit when He comes to live inside of you? A fully devoted "yes" to Christ's transforming work will turn your Living Level into a powerful makeover of the soul.

From Learning to Living?

Before we leave this topic, we need to discuss one more important reality about the five levels. You can't skip a personal growth level and move directly to the next one. Each level builds on the one previous, one after another, in a natural progression—with one exception. In some cases, it is possible to cross the Learning Level, skip the Thinking Level, and proceed directly onto the Living Level. How? By placing action steps in your Growth TRAC that don't require you to gain or reflect upon knowledge. Instead, they focus solely on *doing*.

For example, if you formulate a goal to work out four times a week, you don't need to set aside time for "reflective thinking" to accomplish that goal. Certainly you could...but most likely you'd just *do it*. Here's how to know if you can skip the Thinking Level: if your Growth TRAC doesn't include training, resources, or relationships—in other words, it's comprised mainly of experiences—then it may be possible to jump straight to the Living Level.

In cases where reflective thinking isn't necessary before you take action, consider using reflective thinking after you integrate a new behavior into your life. Often, your reflection will be just that: *looking back—after* you've executed your plan. You may want to process what you've been doing, evaluate how well it's working, and consider what adjustments you might want to make going forward.

But most of your Growth TRAC objectives won't fit this model. Many will include a roadmap made up of training (conferences, seminars, workshops), resources (books, blogs, podcasts), and relationships (mentoring, coaching, discipling) that require you to reflect. In almost every case, you're going to need time to reflect on what you've learned, to absorb its truths, *before* you can move forward into actionable steps on the Living Level. And moving to the Living Level requires another GO! Practice. That's where we'll turn our attention next.

_____ *Chapter 8* _____

Tenacious Application: More Than Good Intentions

I f you've ever ventured onto the road of weight loss, you know that half the battle is dropping the weight...but the other half is keeping it off. Most of us are like a yo-yo when it comes to weight loss. We lose 10 pounds, and then gain 10 pounds. Up and down we go, usually netting more *up* than *down*, if you know what I mean. But Brian's story is different, and shows us that it's possible to cut the string on the yo-yo...while it's down.

Brian married Kat in June 1998, and like so many people, Brian started putting on the weight shortly after saying, "I do!" Less than three years later he had ballooned to 270 pounds. That's where his weight loss journey began.

While his marriage was great, Brian admits that almost every other area of his life was in the dump. His relationship with God was non-existent. His motivation for the future was depleted like an overdrawn bank account. His performance at work bottomed out and he was on the verge of losing his job. In Brian's words, "Working in sales from home and having no motivation to do anything was a bad combination." Needless to say, his self-esteem was at an all time low.

Into the middle of this toxic blend of mediocrity and apathy, one of Brian's co-workers issued a challenge. It was a bet to see who could lose the most weight in only three months. The challenge was appealing to Brian because he and Kat were discussing the possibility of starting a family. The thought of being a father too lazy and out of shape to play with his kids scared Brian. Even worse was the fear of dying before the age of 50, leaving Kat to take care of their children...alone. So Brian took up the challenge with a determined, "I'm in."

Brian began by watching what he ate. That might sound like a pre-school answer to a complicated problem, but it was anything but simple for Brian. He cut soft drinks, fast food, and desserts from his diet—not just some of the time, but all of the time. Brian recalls:

> Every party, every cookout, every meal, you have to make a decision. Do you give in or are you going to be strong? I had a long life of training myself to eat and drink junk. You can't just turn that off overnight. So I literally had to take it day by day and meal by meal and make a decision dozens of times per day...am I going to overcome or am I going to give in and be that weak person that allowed himself to get to 270 pounds?

Initially Brian was met with success, losing 15 pounds in the first four weeks of his challenge. But then his efforts turned into a plateau and the idea of losing weight became much more difficult. That's where most people throw in the towel and call it quits. Plateaus are where the lights get turned out on most peoples' dreams. But Brian refused to give up. His gritty resolve to do what was best for he and his family was like a blaring locomotive horn keeping his dreams from drifting to sleep. So when he found himself sitting on a plateau, Brian decided to make *drastic* changes. He might have coasted into his weight gain, but he certainly wasn't going to coast out of it.

A friend recommended to Brian that he read a popular book that outlined a weight loss and workout program. This wasn't one of those gimmicky programs with a magic pill or an overnight success strategy. It was a permanent lifestyle change. Brian changed his attitude about eating, seeing meals as fuel for the body rather than comfort food during the woes of life. He learned how to eat right, cut alcohol from his diet, and started working out six days a week.

Brian admits that it's easy to make excuses for not working out—too busy, too tired, don't feel like it. I'm sure you could add a few of your own excuses to the list too. But once again, Brian made a decision that working out would be one of his highest priorities in life. In Brian's words, "It is non-negotiable. It's no different than taking a shower or brushing my teeth. It's something I'm going to do every day. If that means getting up at 5:00 am (and I'm NOT a morning person), then I get up at 5:00 in the morning. But I could not let the excuses dictate my health." Whether Brian was on the road for a sales meeting or working from his home office, he was (and is) faithful to his workout. No excuses! Period!

With his new diet plan and consistent workout routine, the weight started to disappear again. By the end of the three-month challenge, Brian had dropped 35 pounds. He won the bet. That could have been the end of the road for Brian's health goal. He could have easily chalked it up as a victory and then returned to his comfort food. That's what his co-worker did, eventually gaining all of his weight back. But Brian's success gave him glimpses of a hope-filled future that motivated him to keep going.

Kat cheered Brian on as he tenaciously climbed the weight loss ladder day after day. And Brian's boss—the same one who nearly fired him a few months earlier—became his biggest champion. He supported and coached Brian, constantly reassuring him and telling him how proud he was of Brian's efforts. That constant stream of encouragement was the accountability he needed to stay the course. It helped Brian keep motivated. And even though many of the weight loss experts say you shouldn't weigh in every day, Brian ignored their advice and stepped onto the scale each morning.

"If I messed up one day," Brian said, "I wanted to see the ramifications...and the scale would show me that." Every pound gained was one more reason to get back on track. And every pound lost was one more milestone in the journey to success. But Brian's number one motivator was still his future children. And by the end of the eighth month, Brian had lost 90 pounds.

To Brian's surprise, his growth (or in this case his reduction) led to greater growth in other areas of his life. Not only did his weight loss improve his health, it improved his confidence and performance at work. The same year of his weight loss, Brian won a major sales achievement award for the very first time, winning an all expense paid vacation with his wife. And in the years that have followed, Brian has repeatedly won sales awards and been promoted in the company. But more important than the awards and promotions, Brian's dream of having children is a reality. He and Kat have two beautiful girls. And because he's taking care of his health, two girls will have a lifetime of amazing memories with their daddy.

Brian's story is a reminder that all of us can climb our most difficult mountains. And when we do, the results are like a ripple, inspiring growth and awakening giants in other sleepy areas of our lives. But the climb isn't always easy. As Brian discovered, each step required tenacious, courage-filled application of ideas and practices that could change his life. Brian decided to turn "could" into "would." He closed the gap between *what if* and *what is*. And today his message is simple: "If I can do it, I know you can."

All of us are guilty of dancing around the Living Level of personal growth without fully committing to it. We've learned and we've thought, only to learn some more and think some more. But just like Brian's quest to get in shape and the Wright brothers' vision to fly, eventually we have to make a decision to do something with what we know—to break out of the learning/thinking cycle and choose to act. That's where tension lives. As Dick Biggs once said, "The greatest gap in life is the one between knowing and doing." Unless you close that gap, you'll never experience a personal growth revolution...and you certainly won't inspire one in somebody else. You can keep what you've learned bottled up in your mind like a message lost at sea, or you can uncork what you know with the Go! Practice of the Living Level.

GO! Practice #3: Tenacious Application:
How to Move to the Living Level

So, how do you move to the Living Level of personal growth? It's deceptively, simply obvious—*tenacious application.* Socrates once said, "Let him that would move the world, first move himself." Take stubborn, gritty resolve, scoop up what you've learned, and *do it*. That happens when you put this "action equation" to work:

$$\left[\; \text{Inner Resolve} \times \text{Outer Support} = \text{Tenacious Application} \; \right]$$

Inner resolve combines *conviction* and *courage*, working together to give you inner determination to act with boldness and belief. Outer support is *accountability* and *dependence*, tapping ongoing encouragement and strength beyond ourselves. Multiplying inner resolve with outer support results in you tenaciously applying the things you're learning. Let's unpack each part of the action equation with some definitions:

INNER RESOLVE (CONVICTION AND COURAGE)

Conviction is a deep inner belief that what you are doing is both right and necessary. You can only be tenacious about things you believe in deeply. You'll only apply to your life those ideas, practices, lessons, and behaviors that you genuinely believe are worth your time and effort. Wilbur and Orville Wright's personal growth was far more than just a passing curiosity about aviation. The possibility of human flight was a deep-rooted conviction that led them to tenacious application. And Brian's commitment to lose weight was driven by a deep conviction centered around his future children.

Application without conviction is like an Olympian without heart. Even the most gifted Olympian won't deliver a gold medal if her heart's not in the sport. Conviction is where you'll find the confidence and the commitment you'll need to propel yourself forward. Conviction helps you overcome the temptation to simply allow your old, unproductive habits to remain entrenched in your life like rusty railroad tracks. Conviction drives your reconstruction ambitions, helping you to pry those old tracks out, laying down a new set of habits.

Courage is the backbone to admit you have fears, face them, and act in spite of them. Odds are, you can't apply what you're learning without having to do something new. As we've discussed, it's in our nature to resist change. Doing something new always requires courage...even if it's just a little. *All growth has risk. All growth has an element of uncertainty.* Will you fail? Possibly. Could a misstep take you three steps backward? Maybe. Basketball great Michael Jordan once said: "I've missed more than nine thousand shots in my career. I've lost almost three hundred games. Twenty-six times I've been trusted to take the winning shot and missed. I've failed over and over and over again in my life. And that is why I succeed." Every single time you don't act, fear wins.

> *"I've missed more than nine thousand shots in my career. I've lost almost three hundred games. Twenty-six times I've been trusted to take the winning shot and missed. I've failed over and over and over again in my life. And that is why I succeed."*[45]
> *Michael Jordon*

Tenacious application is stubborn; it refuses to back away from fear. Courage means leaning in, crossing the edges of your comfort zone, just doing whatever it takes to become the person you want to become. It feels emotional—because fear is an emotion. Andy Stanley observes, "Courage is the willingness to move in a direction in spite of the emotions and thoughts that bid you to do otherwise.... Without courage we will simply accumulate a collection of good ideas and regrets."[46] Courage looks right into the eyes of your emotions, sees the fear, and chooses to move forward anyway. Courage refuses to sit down, joining regret and its friends at the table of inaction.

So what does it take to activate courage? One word—*preparation*. Anytime I'm speaking on a new topic, I increase my prep time dramatically. Why? Because I know from experience that without the right amount of preparation, I'll fall flat on my face. But the more I prepare, the more confident I am to speak on a topic. The same is true for you. Your level of preparation at the Learning Level and Thinking Level has a direct bearing on your willingness to act at the Living Level. Do you need additional training before you can move forward? Do you need to read another book? Spend more time with a mentor? If your fears keep paralyzing you, talk to a counselor and get some help. *Preparation won't remove all of your fear, but it will increase your confidence.* The truth is, you'll never feel fully prepared. But you *can* be grossly underprepared.

You might be asking yourself, "But what if I fail?" There's always the chance that you'll courageously attempt to apply something you've learned to your life...and it will backfire. When that happens—and you can be sure that sometimes it will—pick yourself up and keep moving. Success may not follow every act of conviction-filled courage, but you can be sure of one thing...success will *never* follow your retreat to comfort and safety. It's better to find God's grace on the other side of failure than to find His correction on this side of safety.

Don't let the fear of failure derail your pursuit of growth. If you do, you'll only hand the keys of your future over to the landlord of comfort and security. You'll barricade your life inside the walls of routine, where personal growth revolutions die. *Don't be afraid of what might or might not happen if you move to the Living*

Level. Instead, focus on what should happen. Pursue your growth with courage and then reflect on your growth with grace. In other words, face your fears head on, but don't condemn yourself if things don't go exactly the way you planned.

> *Pursue your growth with courage and then reflect on your growth with grace.*

Let the words of Theodore Roosevelt stir you to something great: "Far better it is to dare mighty things, to win glorious triumphs, even though checkered by failure, than to take rank with those poor spirits who neither enjoy much nor suffer much, because they live in the gray twilight that knows not victory nor defeat."[47]

OUTER SUPPORT (ACCOUNTABILITY AND DEPENDENCE)

Accountability is the oven that keeps conviction and courage hot. It's at the Living Level where the accountability part of your Growth **TRAC** provides the greatest support. When a friend, coworker, family member, pastor, or leader holds you accountable, they continually remind you of *why* you're doing what you're doing. That *why* raises the temperature of your conviction. When you're wrestling with how to apply what you're learning to your life, it's often your accountability and growth relationships that provide the missing ingredients that tell you how to make that courageous leap to the Living Level. And when you feel weary in the journey of *doing*, it's these relationships that inspire you, motivate you, and build you up with support and encouragement. That's exactly what Brian's boss did for him. His accountability and encouragement gave Brian the strength to accelerate out of plateaus and keep moving forward.

When you shortchange accountability in your Growth TRAC, you're just going to fall back into old habits that don't work. It's like watching reruns of an old TV show that never made it past the first season. In the end, you're the same person you've always been—a lifetime of reruns.

Dependence is the paradox of surrender bringing strength. Dependence is when I surrender my "I can do it by myself" attitude and lean on God for his strength. Dependence is the intersection of my growth gap with God's grace. No matter how hard I try, my efforts alone are not—and never will be—enough. I need God! And so do you. We

> *Dependence is the intersection of my growth gap with God's grace.*

need the Spirit of Grace. God's grace is what gives us the ability to change. I've already said that only Christ can transform the human heart. But God's transforming power is not limited to the human heart. You need God's help:

To love your spouse

To raise your kids

To live a life of purity

To get in shape physically

To bring your finances into alignment with God's will

To refine your skills on the job

To pursue your educational goals

To develop your emotional intelligence

To overcome addictive behaviors

And that's just the beginning. You can't reach your full missional potential on your own...no matter how good you are. Why would you even try? You have to replace your dependence on yourself with selfless trust in God if you want to set tenacious application in motion. Does that mean all we have to do is ask God for help? That He waves some magic wand over our lives, transforming us in an instant? If only it were that easy! Dependence on God is not a cop-out for our own discipline. Instead, dependence gives us the power to be disciplined.

Both conviction and courage grow from within. Accountability and dependence come from outside. Both combinations work together as an *action equation*—producing tenacious application—to help you develop new habits and actually do what you already know you should be doing. When you put the action equation to work in your life, not only will you see progress, but you'll also develop consistency in the regular and constant application of what you're learning. You'll cultivate healthy, ongoing habits, not just one-time wins.

Now it's time to step into the Living Level. Answer the following questions. Each question is built around the GO! Practice of tenacious application:

- Do you truly believe—have a deep conviction—that you need to apply what you've learned to your life? If so, reflect on that conviction and let it settle deep within your soul. If not, be honest with yourself and stop beating yourself up over inaction in this area.
- What's the first courageous step you need to take to apply what you've learned to your life? Do you need to spend more time in preparation before you take that first step? If so, how (specifically) do you need to prepare?
- Who can hold you accountable to take the first step to apply what you've learned?
- Are you depending on God to help you change? What do you need to surrender? How do you need God to help you? Pray now. Make your commitment to God, and ask Him for His help and strength.

From Tenacious Application
to Personal Transformation

Tenacious application is the **GO! PRACTICE** of the **Living Level of personal growth.** It means having not only the conviction about what to do, but also the courage to actually do it consistently. It means being honest enough to realize that you need help from God and from others. But it's all worth it, because **The OUTCOME** of this practice is *personal transformation.*

After years of learning and thinking, the Wright brothers took the bold risk of action. Their risk first transformed them personally, and then went on to influence the skyline of the entire planet. Brian's tenacious application in the area of weight loss produced personal transformation on multiple fronts—physically, emotionally, at work, and with his family. What about you? Which areas of discovery are you still waiting to translate into meaningful action? Why are you holding back? *Unless you take the risk of application, you can never experience the rewards of transformation.* Without risk, you'll become nothing more than an expert in regret.

Colleen Barrett of Southwest Airlines once said, "When it comes to getting things done, we need fewer architects and more bricklayers." You didn't design a Growth TRAC so that you could frame it with inaction and admire it with regret. You designed a Growth TRAC to lead you to spiritual, mental, relational, and physical bricklaying.

> *"When it comes to getting things done, we need fewer architects and more bricklayers." Colleen Barrett*

For your *tenacious application* to result in *personal transformation*, you must consistently take what you've learned and put it to work in your life. Your spiritual health needs more than one devotional time with God. Your physical health requires more than a single workout. Your professional growth means not only courageously implementing new strategies, but also monitoring and refining those strategies over time. The health of your family requires consistent relational time, not just an annual vacation. Don't just muster the courage to act once. Instead, cultivate the correct habits to sustain personal change.

The Living Level is where you do or die. In fact, the five levels of personal growth are really riding on what happens at the Living Level. The Living Level is the hinge on which the other levels swing. If you *learn it* and *think it* but never cross that magic line of *doing it*, you've just wasted all that investment. As Henry Ford once said, "You can't build a reputation on what you are going to do." Good intentions mean nothing without action. That's why *tenacious application requires conviction and courage from within, the supporting accountability from others, and dependence on God.* Only then can you experience personal transformation.

Baby Steps

All of this may sound exhilarating and exhausting. While we all dream about personal transformation, most of us are all too familiar with the setbacks that come with it. That's why it's good to remind yourself that before you can run, you have to walk. Before you can walk, you have to take some baby steps. Here are three baby steps that will help you actually see progress at the Living Level:

1. Identify **ONE** simple action step – You may have spent a lot of time learning and thinking. If you're having trouble translating everything you've learned into action, then just keep it

really simple. Boil everything down to ONE simple action step. The more complicated an action step is, the more fear it's capable of producing. ***Simplicity reduces fear.***

2. WRITE OUT your first action step – Writing always increases clarity because it forces you to shape your thoughts into actionable words. If you can't write out an action step in one (or at the most two) simple sentences, then you don't yet have clarity about how to apply what you've learned. Keep pushing yourself until you can articulate the action step on paper to the point that you will have zero confusion about precisely what to do next. ***Writing produces clarity.***

3. GO PUBLIC with a time-bound version of your first action step – Find a friend, or even a group of friends, and share the action step you're planning to take. Share your deadline, too. Really talk it up big. When you go public like this, you're putting yourself on the line to actually do what you said you would do. Your friends will inevitably bring it up again in the future. You might even ask them to hold you accountable. ***Going public helps you conquer procrastination.***

These baby steps are no guarantee. But they'll definitely help you reach beyond your overwhelming feelings of inaction. It's fine to make mistakes when you take baby steps. Babies fall again and again before they suddenly take off walking. But they keep trying. Remember, if you'll embrace the courage to *grow* with a spirit of *grace*, you'll be well on your way to applying what you've learned.

Disturbed

Several years ago Karen and I vacationed for a few days in Washington, D.C. Every time I visit our nation's capital, the sheer magnitude and design of the sites there always leaves me awestruck. Climbing the steps to the Lincoln Memorial reminds me, every time, of Martin Luther King, Jr.'s "I Have a Dream" speech. Walking among the Korean, Vietnam, and World War II Memorials always humbles me, as I think of the countless sacrifices they represent. The details in the architectural designs of the US Capitol, the Supreme Court, and the Library of Congress grip my imagination. Every time I go to D.C., I just expect to be overwhelmed. But nothing could have prepared me for my first visit to the Holocaust Memorial Museum.

I find fascinating things to study in every museum, but limited time always requires you to be selective. There's always plenty of "stuff" that I'd just as soon walk right past. That's how I treat most museum visits: show me the good stuff, and I'll leave the rest for people who have more time than they know what to do with. The Holocaust Memorial Museum was the polar opposite.

The moment I walked into that museum, I was ensnared, mesmerized by everything around me. I floated from one display to another, gripped by every photo, engrossed in every word describing the Jews' dreadful journey through destruction. Not a single element was "wasted." When I snapped awake, I saw I had already spent a full hour in what felt like minutes. I realized I wasn't going to finish the museum experience—packed with more than 900 artifacts and 70 video monitors—unless I could accelerate my pace.

I remember wandering into a railcar that had been used to transport Jews to their deaths. I remember the smell of the shoes of the victims. I can still picture the "Tower of Faces"— a three-floor-high wall of photos towering above my head— moms and dads, sons and daughters, representing the Jewish community of the Lithuanian town of Eisiskes. Eisiskes' Jewish population was combined together with the Jewish communities of two neighboring towns, Valkininkas and Salcininkai, and more than 4,000 men, women, and children were massacred at the murderous hands of hate. Only 29 Jews escaped.

During one of our visits to the museum, a Holocaust survivor who worked there showed me, Karen, and Ashley the concentration camp number permanently imprinted on his arm. A living history book stood right there in front of us, pouring out his personal firsthand experience of the horrors of *his* Holocaust. We were all moved. We were all changed.

The Holocaust Memorial Museum is filled with stories, sights, and sounds like these, that seize your soul. One is a simple, unsettling quote: "Thou shalt not be a victim. Thou shalt not be a perpetrator. Above all, thou shalt not be a bystander." That last word—"bystander"—particularly disturbs me. A bystander is a spectator. In the case of the Holocaust, a spectator is a spineless eyewitness to evil. How can you be "just a bystander" to the extermination of six million innocent people?

A Different Kind of Bystander

It's hard for most of us to imagine ourselves in that role: a bystander to reprehensible acts of genocide. We don't believe we could be lulled into what we perceive as callous, merciless inaction. But the truth is, every one of us has a kind of bystander living inside us. Being inside, it's much more subtle, more acceptable. We take a passive stance, turning a blind eye to our God-given potential, a deaf ear to God's call to grow, to change, and to be transformed.

We conveniently ignore our own disconnect, the one that exists between what we've learned and how we know we should live. As one man said, "Most of us are educated far beyond our own obedience." It's so easy to allow our quest for information to produce nothing more than educated inaction. Not only is that useless and pointless—it's irresponsible! What's the point in learning and thinking, only to do nothing?

When personal growth turns into a spectator sport—never moving to the Living Level, where true change occurs—we passively allow a part of ourselves to die, making us participants in a terrible annihilation. ***Choosing not to act on what we've learned is exactly that: a choice.*** We sit and wait, often justifying our inaction, saying things like, "I'm waiting on the Lord to speak to me," or "I'm really busy now. When things slow down I'll start acting on what I've learned." We're fat and happy—constipated by our intake of knowledge with no corresponding outflow of action. (Too much? Maybe. But isn't it true?)

You might say, "Who cares? It's my life. If I don't want to act on things I learn, that's my own business. I'm not hurting anybody." Actually, that's not true. (We'll talk about that in the next chapter.) But even if it were true, why would you want to live that way? Why would you want to sign a death warrant for your own potential, just because you're too lazy or unwilling to turn your learning into living? I'll be honest: It's not easy. The Living Level isn't comfy box seats. To truly live, you can't simply watch the action and play armchair quarterback. Your life is your game. You need to get in it. The Living Level is out there on the field, where your sweat, discipline, responsibility, and perseverance move your life down the field.

Let the Living Level become the hinge of your personal growth. Have more than good intentions. Revolt against the bystander inside of you. Tenaciously apply what you're learning, and you'll experience a personal growth revolution greater than you've ever known. When you do, you'll find yourself on the doorstep of the fourth level of personal growth—*Impacting.*

GO! Starting a Personal Growth Revolution				
GO! Practice	Activates	Level of Personal Growth	Which results in	Outcome
Growth TRACing	⟶	The Learning Level	⟶	Growth Traction
Reflective Thinking	⟶	The Thinking Level	⟶	Mental Maturity
Tenacious Application	⟶	The Living Level	⟶	Personal Transformation

Chapter 9

The Impacting Level: Moving Beyond Yourself

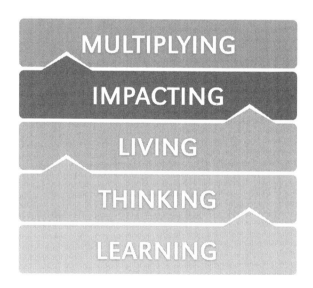

want you to imagine for a moment that at an early age you set up a financial account with one goal: to add something, any-thing, to the account *every day*. You open your account with a $100 deposit and your journey begins.

Every day you make a deposit. Sometimes your deposit is large—like on paydays or when you get an unexpected bonus or gift. But most of the time, your deposit is fairly small. Some days you deposit five bucks while other days you deposit only a dollar. Your goal isn't the amount of the deposit, but that you actually make a deposit *every* day.

Your daily routine slowly begins to add up. Each month when you get your financial statement, you're encouraged by your progress. After your first year, your account has $1,200 in it. You quickly do the math and realize that after making your initial $100 deposit, and collecting a little bit of interest, you've averaged roughly $3 per day in deposits. You're happy with your progress, but you know you can do better. So as your second year begins, you bring a bit more discipline to your finances, and you allocate as much as possible to your daily habit.

Day after day you make your deposit. Sometimes it's a real inconvenience. Some days you're tired from working late and just don't want to deal with the hassle. Some days you're sick, other days you're buried in house chores, and some days you simply don't care. But you made a commitment and you refuse to quit. You make your deposit day after day, week after week, month after month, and year after year.

Your savings grow throughout the years—as does the amount you're able to deposit each day—and you're encouraged by the results you see from compound interest. As the stash gets bigger, you begin to dream about all the possibilities your future holds. You think about the vacations you can take, the stuff you can buy, but more than anything, you dream about the contributions you can make in your community and world.

Your heart is stirred when you see images of poverty, hear stories from missionaries, and see the education gaps in younger generations. Sometimes you're even tempted to withdraw some of the money so that you can help somebody in need. But you don't. You convince yourself that if you leave the money alone, it will keep growing, and then one day you'll be able to make a really big difference.

As you approach retirement years, you've accumulated an enormous amount of money. Daily deposits with zero withdrawals have produced enough money to retire very comfortably and to fulfill your dreams of helping people in need. But something else has happened during this time. As your money has grown, so have your insecurities. Instead of using what you've accumulated to make a dent in poverty, invest in missions, and address educational needs, you feel overwhelmed by the enormity of the problems. Despair sets in as you realize that while you're money has grown, so have the size of the problems in society. So you leave your money alone...hoping it will grow a little bit more.

Although your financial picture has improved over the years, your life has not been easy. Your spouse passed away sooner than expected. And because you never had kids, you're now alone. You are ravaged with regrets as you replay your life...wondering what could have been. Fear sets in. Your mind torments you. You become bitter, jaded, and absorbed with self-pity.

Your rapidly failing health leads you to make a rash, almost unfathomable decision. You withdraw every dollar from your account and revise your will with one incredibly stupid line: "Bury all of my money with me." Life ends...and your legacy of selfishness begins.

Dead Growth

Anybody in their right mind knows that going to your grave with your investments—literally—is foolish. And yet, it happens every day. No, people are not being buried with millions of dollars of cash in their casket. They're being buried with something even more valuable.

Day after day, week after week, month after month people make daily deposits into the account of their personal growth. They read, learn, study, and acquire valuable learning experiences. With discipline and faithfulness, they make small, simple daily deposits into their growth. Those deposits compound over time and they begin to enjoy the benefits of years of personal growth.

With each deposit they dream about the person they can become and even think about how they might help others grow, too. Despite their wonderful learning posture, their insecurities, fears, and feelings of inadequacy hold them back. Rather than investing in somebody else's growth, they simply stockpile their own. They're like a library with no visitors.

As life comes to an end, they selfishly take their growth with them to the grave. It is permanently lost. Why? They never made withdrawals from all of those personal growth deposits to invest in somebody else. What was learned, thought, and lived, was ultimately lost. Their growth died with them.

The point isn't to stop growing so that you can help others grow. The point is to keep growing *and* start giving. That's the only way to leave a personal growth legacy. If you want to leave a legacy worth remembering when you die, you have to write a legacy worth recording while you're alive. To pass that legacy on to future generations, you must write it not only on your life, but on the lives of the people you influence too. That's where the Impacting Level is different—here personal growth turns *outward* and you begin inspiring a personal growth revolution in others.

Jared's Story

Years ago Jared Fogle appeared on TV after his amazing weight loss journey with the Subway restaurant chain. Affectionately dubbed "Jared the Subway Guy," Jared Fogle was—and is—admired for overcoming the battle of the bulge. So what exactly is the story behind Jared's success?

In March, 1998, Jared was a college student at Indiana University. He was severely overweight—a problem he developed in adolescence—and his health was rapidly deteriorating. Jared's father is a physician, and his own prognosis of Jared's health was gloomy: "Dead by 40!" Changing his life was a monumental task. He didn't need to drop 20 pounds—those proverbial love handles that so many of us have. Jared needed to drop more than 200 pounds. Tipping the scales at 425 pounds and wearing pants with a 60-inch waistline, his obesity was destroying his life. Some days Jared was eating 10,000 calories, enough for five people.

Jared finally stopped procrastinating, chunked his file cabinet full of excuses, and got tenacious...*really tenacious.* Next door to Jared's apartment building was a Subway restaurant. While he frequently ate at Subway, it wasn't until Jared was at his heaviest weight that he noticed a sign advertising "7 for 6" (seven sandwiches with six grams of fat or less). So Jared made a drastic shift in his diet—he decided to eat two Subway sandwiches every day...*for an entire year.*

Now, I don't know about you, but eating at the same restaurant every day for a week is bad enough...*but for a year?* It sounds like a modern day version of the Children of Israel eating manna in the desert. But that's what Jared did.

With each passing week, the weight came off—10 pounds, 20 pounds, 50 pounds, 80 pounds. After dropping 125 pounds, just by changing his eating habits, Jared started exercising too—walking to class instead of riding the bus. By the time Jared weighed 250 pounds, he walked everywhere, roughly one and a half miles per day.

Jared's weight loss wasn't an overnight miracle or the result of some magic pill. It was a process—day-by-day, week-by-week, and month-by-month. It was one disciplined, tenacious action step after another. Jared's inner resolve, combined with encouragement and accountability from his family and a college friend, produced amazing results. In just under twelve months, and 700 Subway sandwiches later, Jared lost a total of 245 pounds.

The Subway® restaurant chain heard about Jared's incredible story from an article in Indiana University's campus newspaper. Subway decided to defy the conventional wisdom that a person couldn't lose weight by eating fast food. Jared was their proof. So they invited Jared to appear in their commercials for an ad campaign. The results? Sales immediately jumped by nearly 20 percent.[48]

160,000 Pounds Later

Since Jared's commercials first aired, thousands of letters, photos, and e-mails have poured into Subway's corporate headquarters from people who lost weight after seeing and hearing Jared's inspiring story. How much weight? So far those who shared their stories have lost a combined total of 160,000 pounds. Do you know how much 160,000 pounds is? It's equal to:

- 14,545 skateboards
- 10,000 Marching band Tubas
- 842 Jareds
- 492 Black Bears
- 426 Gorillas
- 184 Grand Pianos[49]

Even after a 40 pound hiccup at the end of 2009, Jared refused to let himself spiral out of control. Today, Jared maintains a weight of 190 pounds. He shares his story all over the world and has appeared on major network talk shows. He started a foundation to fight childhood obesity, and he's spoken to tens of thousands of children, challenging them to eat healthy and exercise regularly.

Jared is experiencing the five levels of personal growth in a truly remarkable way. For Jared, that started by *learning* how to take care of his health along with a radical departure from his normal way of *thinking* about food and exercise. His new way of thinking led to a new way of *living.* Jared changed. And because Jared changed, he started *impacting* others. Therein lies an important truth about the Impacting Level: **None of us can positively change what's happening around us unless we're first willing to change ourselves.**

You'll never "arrive" when it comes to personal growth—it really is a lifelong process. Strengths can always get stronger, liabilities can always be shored up, and new roles and opportunities always require new growth. Yet as you continue the personal growth journey, and enjoy the benefits of seeing your growth compound, you can't stop at the Living Level. Why would you want to stop prematurely when your greatest potential for impact is still before you?

Inspiring a Personal Growth Revolution

At the Impacting Level of personal growth, everything turns outward. **Not only do you experience a personal growth revolution, but you inspire a growth revolution in others' too.** Your growth deposits become the fuel to influence others to grow.

That's exactly what Jared has done through his involvement with Subway. His story of personal transformation is impacting thousands of people. The Subway website is filled with testimonies from people who were inspired by Jared's story and found the courage to tackle their own weight problem. As a result, many of them have lost significant amounts of weight and turned their health around.

Through Jared's disciplined commitment to personal growth, he moved beyond solely *learning, thinking,* and *living.* Today he is *impacting.* You might say, "Well if I had a national fast food chain endorsing me, I could impact others as well." But I believe Jared would impact people whether or not Subway ever used him in a commercial. He FIRST lost the 245 pounds. And his tenacious action inspired people BEFORE he was ever seen on TV.

Think about it—if you were severely overweight and you lost 245 pounds in one year, wouldn't those closest to you take note? Wouldn't they raise their eyebrows and ask you what your secret was? Wouldn't your powerful example inspire them to lose weight too? You would be motivated to use your remarkable transformation to help other people achieve their full potential.

Jesus said, "You don't get wormy apples off a healthy tree, nor good apples off a diseased tree. The health of the apple tells the health of the tree. You must begin with your own life-giving lives. It's who you are, not what you say and do, that counts. *Your true being brims over into true words and deeds*"[50] (emphasis added). The Impacting Level is not about what you can get or how you can grow, but rather how your life can *brim over with words and deeds* to help others grow. It's "output from the overflow." In other words, it's impacting others—output—from the overflow of your own personal growth reservoir. Everything you've deposited in your personal growth account at the Learning, Thinking, and Living Levels brims over into words and deeds that inspire growth in the people around you.

Characteristics of the Impacting Level

In the last couple of chapters I emphasized that the Living Level is the hinge on which the other levels swing. Before the Living Level you engage in growth preparation. During it you embrace growth application. After it you embark on growth cultivation in others. The focus shifts at the Impacting Level, encompassing more than your own personal missional potential. It requires you to think selflessly about personal growth. It requires a firm resolve to not go to your grave with your personal growth still inside of you. This level is marked by three unique qualities: Your life is a model for others to follow; you are intentional about helping others grow; and others show growth as a result of your influence.

YOUR LIFE IS A MODEL FOR OTHERS TO FOLLOW

All of us have heard the phrase, "lead by example." It's a cliché that's often overstated yet under practiced. It's no secret that an ethical gap exists in our culture—from the big screen in Hollywood to the halls of power in Washington D.C. The faith in corporate America has plummeted as stories of CEO and corporate abuse have ravaged the headlines. However, the ethical lapse does not exist solely in the corner office or in the influential segments of society. Fifty-six percent of employees have observed some form of ethical misconduct in the workplace.

This knowing-doing gap is what keeps so many people from moving to the Impacting Level of personal growth. Why? Because at the Impacting Level, your life is a model that others seek to emulate. Who wants to imitate a glaring behavior gap? People are inspired by consistently positive behavior born out of the depth of your character, integrity, and spirituality. Your Achilles' heel won't inspire anyone.

At the Impacting Level, you have the extraordinary opportunity to model behavior that others *want* to follow. Instead of demanding that your kids, employees, and volunteers follow you, they readily do so at the Impacting Level because your model of behavior has earned their trust. When you silently model the right behaviors, you teach others loud and clear. Matthew Henry, the great theologian of the early 1700s, asserted, "Those who teach by their doctrine must teach by their life, or else they pull down with one hand what they build up with the other."[51]

Your behavior is a model—a powerful catalyst—that can inspire transformation in people around you. The Apostle Paul was so confident in his personal model that he said, "Follow my example, as I follow the example of Christ."[52] You might not be a "Paul," but I'll bet there's something in your life worth imitating. If you were going to make a list of qualities, skills, habits, and attitudes from your own life that you would want others to emulate, what would your list look like?

YOU ARE INTENTIONAL ABOUT HELPING OTHERS GROW

The second characteristic of the Impacting Level reveals an elevation in personal responsibility—you're *intentional* about helping others grow. Because individualism and privacy are so ingrained in our culture, it's easy to neglect opportunities to invest in others' growth. The last thing we want to do is come across as pushy or get up in someone's business, so we tend to swing to the other extreme and back off completely. But you also can't take your personal growth with you to the grave. So understand this: the Impacting Level is about investing in people, not intimidating them. Your goal is not to make people feel uncomfortable or to be some know-it-all who has come to save the day. The focus is simply to—in a natural and nonintrusive way—intentionally use your personal growth to help others grow too. At the Impacting Level, you move from accelerating growth within you to accelerating growth around you.

> At the Impacting Level, you move from accelerating growth within you to accelerating growth around you.

Your intentionality in helping others grow—whether it's your family, fellow employees, friends, volunteers, neighbors, or somebody in need—is directly tied to three things: *potential*, *needs*, and *deposits*.

Potential. Every person you encounter has potential. Some people aggressively pursue their full potential, others are blinded to their potential, and still others are concerned about only one thing: survival. The real question at the Impacting Level is this: can you see the potential in the people around you? You're not very likely to invest in someone's growth if you don't believe in who they can become.

Needs. When you interact with others, you'll also discover their capacity gaps—those missing links between who they are and who they have the potential to become. These gaps really represent specific needs. Whether we admit it or not, all of us have needs that require insight, coaching, resources, and encouragement from others so that we can reach our full potential. Some people are facing needs so big—starvation, abuse, · poverty, illiteracy, and disease—that they cannot even think about their potential until these basic human needs are met. At the Impacting Level, you peer into the potential lying deep within a person, and then identify the need—big or small—that's separating that person from becoming everything God created them to be. Only then can you do something to help them close their gap.

Deposits. Once you're aware of a person's potential and discover their needs, make a withdrawal from your account. Rather than hoarding everything you've learned, reach deep into your personal growth reservoir and pull out the right nugget to deposit into their life. That's how you'll help somebody else close his growth gaps. In fact, you are most likely to help others grow in the areas where you have personally grown the most. Your deposit is an investment in their future...a gap-filler that unlocks their missional potential. When you intentionally make these deposits, you're living at the Impacting Level of personal growth.

Are you attuned to the *potential* and *needs* of the people around you? Do you know which *deposits* you have to offer that will help them grow the most? Take a moment and reflect on the deposits you feel best equipped to make. Your deposits should flow out of who you are, how God wired you, how God has blessed you, and the areas in life where you've grown the most. Some of the deposits I feel best equipped to make focus on honing leadership skills, life purpose coaching, personal Growth TRACing, and increasing ministry effectiveness. Why? Because these are the areas where my personal growth account is the largest. What about you? What are the deposits that flow directly from your strengths, abilities, skills, passions, and resources?

OTHERS SHOW GROWTH AS A RESULT OF YOUR INFLUENCE

Entrepreneur and author Regi Campbell has a God-given gift to grow businesses and use his faith to make a difference in the marketplace. As a young Christian, Regi and his wife volunteered to lead a singles ministry in their church. It grew rapidly, and before long Regi was consumed with meetings as he invested in single men who were looking for practical advice. Feeling exhausted and wearing himself ragged, Regi heard Tim Elmore, an author and speaker committed to investing in young leaders, make this statement: "More time with fewer people equals greater kingdom impact." That phrase started a journey for Regi that culminated in what he calls *Next Generation Mentoring.*

"More time with fewer people equals greater kingdom impact."

Since 2000, Regi has strategically invited a group of eight young business executives to join him at his home for a mentoring experience. The group meets once per month for twelve months and is committed to reading books, sharing their takeaways, memorizing Scriptures, praying together, and holding one another accountable. His mentoring process isn't rocket science. It's simply a clear strategy Regi has developed to leverage his personal growth to impact younger leaders.

In 2009, Regi published his ideas in a book titled, *Mentor Like Jesus*. He records the names of each of his mentees in his book and then he makes this observation:

> In the past eight years, I've intentionally mentored sixty-four guys. Most report that they have a deeper, more meaningful walk with Jesus than they did before the next generation mentoring experience. They are disciples...learners and followers of Jesus. To my knowledge none have fallen away. All are still married. All are involved in a church. All are attempting to raise their kids in the faith. And from what I can tell, they are, to varying degrees, walking with God.[53]

These sixty-four men have grown as a result of Regi's influence. He simply took his knowledge in the areas where he has grown the most, and intentionally invested it into a group of guys whom he was best equipped to help. He saw their potential, understood their needs, and knew what kind of deposit he could withdraw and invest into their lives. As a result, he's helped start a personal growth revolution in 64 men.

You can do the same thing Regi did. Maybe it won't be a mentoring group, but you can take the areas where you've grown the most and use them to impact somebody else. Each one of us has influence—even if only with a small handful of people. In fact,

Dr. Tim Elmore points out that sociologists believe the most introverted people in the world will influence an average of 10,000 people during their lifetime.[54] You might influence your family, a small group of friends, or even an entire division in your company. The question isn't "how many" but "how intentionally." How intentionally are you helping others grow? Are you using your influence to deliberately unlock peoples' potential? When you do, you'll experience the power of the Impacting Level.

Who Will You Impact?

One of the greatest joys in life is helping somebody win. When you make a deposit into the bank account of somebody's future, it just feels right. It's like being a gardener, adding water and fertilizer in the flowerbed of somebody's God-inspired dreams. Every deposit you make enriches the soil to maximize their potential.

Take a moment to write down the names of three people who you believe you can impact. These should be people who you believe you can help grow spiritually, mentally, relationally, or physically. They are individuals who can benefit from the "gold" in your own personal growth account. They may be people who you have something in common with such as work, a hobby, or a similar area of interest. Be sure at least one name is somebody from outside of your family.

1. _____
2. _____
3. _____

In the next chapter, I'll share with you the GO! Practice of the Impacting Level. This practice will show you how—on a very practical level—to make growth deposits into your three people listed above.

What makes the Impacting Level so great is that rather than receiving personal growth, you inspire it in others. Rather than celebrating your own growth, you get to celebrate others' growth. This growth represents the *fruit of your influence* in their lives as you've partnered with the work God is doing within them. As Jesus said, "The fruit tells you about the tree."[55]

Don't take your personal growth with you to your grave. Don't keep your lifelong learning a secret. Pry the hands of fear and insecurity off of the investments you've made in your growth. Resist the temptation to hoard your own growth, never making withdrawals that you can deposit in somebody else's growth. Turn your growth *outward*. When you do, you'll reach the Impacting Level of personal growth and you'll begin inspiring a growth revolution around you.

Chapter 10

Intentional Investing: Inspiring Others' Growth

It's no secret that the neighborhoods of inner city America are experiencing the ravaging affects of crime and poverty. Unemployment and poverty rates in America's inner cities are more than double that of the surrounding population, and their median household incomes average half that of surrounding areas.[56] Scores of people have washed their hands of the inner city, choosing to ignore the downward spiral of these central city areas with 100,000+ populations. Businesses have closed up shop and moved to the "burbs" where money and prominence are in greater supply. Even churches have uprooted themselves from the inner city—replacing Christ's mission with "The American Dream"—and found new, more "comfortable" places to minister.

While most people would just as soon take a one-way ticket out of the inner city, Bill Strickland has made it his mission, focusing his revolutionary efforts on the inner city of Pittsburgh, Pennsylvania. Strickland is the President and CEO of Manchester Bidwell Corporation and its subsidiaries Manchester

Craftsmen's Guild (MCG) and Bidwell Training Center (BTC). As a visionary and entrepreneurial leader, Strickland brings hope to the inner city by delivering educational opportunities in the arts and providing training for low-income residents. His innovative initiatives are reshaping the business of social change and bringing renewal to urban communities.

Through MCG Youth's in-school, after-school, and summer studio art programs, 3,900 young people each year learn valuable skills in ceramics, photography, digital imaging, and design art. Strickland says, "Entrepreneurs are, by definition, visionaries. The use of art to change students' attitudes is at the heart of my vision of education."[57] Through MCG, Strickland is doing more than mentoring students in art...he's mentoring students in life.

Strickland's ambitions aren't just pie in the sky. In fact, an independent analysis shows that he's reaching his goal. Strickland's programs, offered at no charge to Pittsburgh's Public School students, are changing the environment of the inner city. Students who participate in the MCG programs from nearby David B. Oliver High School—Strickland's alma mater—miss fewer days of school and have a higher grade point average. Incredibly, more than 90% of the students involved in the after-school art program graduate high school, and 85% have gone on to college or enrolled in some form of higher education. And of the adults graduating from BTC's vocational program, 86% find employment.[58]

Transformational Vision

Bill Strickland's vision for inner city transformation knows no end. His vision is like a snowball—with every turn it gets bigger and the opportunities to change lives reaches further. For example, Strickland's devotion to the arts expanded when he started MCG Jazz, launched a recording label, and opened a 350-seat music hall in Pittsburgh. Over 300 Jazz CDs have been recorded—four of which are Grammy Award winners—with many artists returning proceeds to further the mission of the school: to preserve, present, and promote jazz. Through the educational programs of MCG Jazz, inner city students attend concerts, artists offer classes, and marketing and production internships are available.

For over 40 years, the Bidwell Training Center has changed the lives of disadvantaged and dislocated residents. They're not some flash-in-the-pan operation—here today and gone tomorrow—leaving a mess for somebody else to clean up. They understand the needs of the inner city and recognize that change does not happen overnight. Since its inception, BTC has launched diploma majors in high-demand careers with the help of corporate partners who not only assist with the development of BTC majors but also hire BTC graduates. The 163,000 square foot campus isn't some stale educational complex with "Boredom 101" as it's highest attended class. It's a place where vision oozes out of its staff and into the souls of its students. It's a refuge from the streets, an oasis of peace, and a life-giving environment where students' potential is awakened and fresh vision is born. It's a place where Bill Strickland brought to life the words of his mother, Evelyn, that echo in his mind from his childhood: "Just because we're poor, we don't have to live like defeated people."[59] For many, BTC is their only beacon of hope.

Strickland is intentionally investing in people, and he's using his influence to transform the inner city. There's no question that he's made his mark and that his legacy will outlive him. Most people with a resume as long as Strickland's would start thinking about retirement. Not Bill! He refuses to coast on past success. He's a visionary at heart and as long as he's breathing, he'll be dreaming. There are just too many problems waiting to be solved and needs crying to be met. As Winifred Newman once said, "Vision is the world's most desperate need. There are no hopeless situations, only people who think hopelessly." And Bill Strickland is the furthest thing from a hopeless thinker.

Today, Bill's dream is to replicate Manchester Bidwell Corporation's model in 200 urban areas across the country and around the world. He doesn't just want to change one life or bring hope to one community...*he wants to change the world.* And he just might do it.

Are Strickland's efforts inspiring? Absolutely! Are they remarkable? There's no doubt that they are. But *none* of it was possible—not the training center, not the art programs, not the recording label or the music hall—without the extraordinary investment of one man...Frank Ross.

Meet Frank Ross

When Bill Strickland was only 16 years old, he had a simple yet profound encounter that changed the course of his life. As a kid growing up in Manchester, a neighborhood in Pittsburgh, Bill faced the daily struggles of the inner city. Manchester was riddled with dilapidated housing, vacant lots overtaken by weeds, graffiti, abandoned cars, and desperate feelings of hopelessness. Every morning on the way to school, Bill passed drug dealers, predators, scam artists, and hookers. Manchester was the victim of manufacturing shut downs that led to employment loss and the rapid decline of property values. After a new highway bypass was built, connecting downtown Pittsburgh with Ohio River Boulevard, commuter traffic stopped flowing through Manchester and local businesses dried up. As a result, this once working-class community turned into a ghetto filled with despair, crime, and widespread drug use.

As desperate as the situation was in Manchester, Strickland says that he didn't know any different. "I had fallen for the deadliest lie the ghetto uses to shrink your soul—that *your* world is the *whole* world, that your future, and all the sorry possibilities life will ever offer you, are already right before your eyes."[60] More than a location, Strickland was the victim of a mindset.

Bored with school, Bill found himself one Wednesday walking aimlessly through the hallways of Oliver High School. On that September day, he caught a whiff of coffee brewing in the art room. When he peered inside, he was captivated by the sunlight, pouring through the classroom windows like a waterfall teeming over a rugged cliff. His ears were filled with the sounds of jazz music. And a man with long hair and a short beard was hunched over a potter's wheel bringing to life a lump of clay.

As he walked into the classroom, Frank Ross, a ceramics teacher at Oliver High School, looked up and said, "Mr. Strickland, how have you been?" Bill had Mr. Ross for a photography class when he was a sophomore. He liked Mr. Ross because he not only had a passion for his work, but also treated students with respect. Bill's inquisitive mind was racing as he watched Mr. Ross shape a lump of wet clay into a vase.

Perceiving his curiosity, Frank invited Bill to try his hand at the potter's wheel. That was all it took. Like a sleeping giant, something woke up inside of his heart. Bill was instantly hooked, so he signed-up for the class during his senior year.

That encounter was the beginning of a relationship that changed Strickland's life. Mr. Ross began teaching him how to mold clay. Every session behind the potter's wheel was an opportunity to mentor Bill. As clay was taking shape in the hands of a potter, so too was the young life of Bill Strickland. Frank invited him to his home for meals, gave him a key to his house, took him to concerts, and shared his music collection with him. Bill was only 16 years old, but he dreamed of becoming like his new mentor.

More Than a Hobby

Frank Ross was doing more than teaching ceramic lessons; he was teaching life. The potter's wheel wasn't just a random hobby or an extra credit in school—it was a launching pad to create life change. Ross simply used his ceramic skills as a way to influence a young student on the verge of flunking out of school—a student full of potential. He regularly made deposits in Bill's personal growth and came alongside him with the encouragement and support he needed to succeed.

When Strickland graduated from high school in 1967, Ross helped him make the leap into college. It was a big step, but Frank knew the potential for greatness couldn't be wasted. Bill's SAT scores were low, so he entered the University of Pittsburgh on a provisional basis. But with the support of Mr. Ross—that constant coach of encouragement cheering from the sidelines—Bill rose to the occasion and landed on the dean's list.

Today Bill Strickland has been recognized with appointments to national councils and committees, summons from two U.S. Presidents to meet at the White House to discuss his work, ten honorary PhDs, and partnerships with major corporations such as IBM, Alcoa, Heinz, Hewlett-Packard, and Bayer...just to name a few.

Yeah But...

It's really easy to read the story of somebody like Bill Strickland and quickly write yourself off with an emphatic, "Yeah but, I could *never* do that!" Perhaps you're right. Maybe your situation is worse than the inner city of Pittsburgh. Maybe you're living in a hellhole filled with brokenness and despair. Perhaps your capacity doesn't match a dream as big as Bill's.

I don't know your situation or the capacity God created in you. But I do know this: You can do *something* to help *somebody*. You can turn your eyes off of yourself and accelerate growth in somebody around you. You might not be a Bill Strickland, but I'll bet you're a Frank Ross waiting to happen in somebody's life. Will you make the investment in that young Bill Strickland who lives down the street from you or sits in the cubicle next to you? Somebody in your life is franticly looking for the very thing you have to offer.

Because of Frank Ross's influence, a personal growth revolution began inside of Bill Strickland. He became a lifelong learner. He read the books that Ross recommended to him and spent countless hours behind the potter's wheel honing his skills. When his initial efforts in the Manchester neighborhood started to grow, Strickland says, "I had no choice but to grow with it. And that meant developing my leadership and management skills, often on the fly."[61] That growth attitude spilled over into the organizations he leads. One of Manchester Craftsmen's Guild's core values is all about embracing learning opportunities. Strickland has truly modeled the way—closing the gap between who he was and who he could become. And Frank Ross made it all possible by climbing to the Impacting Level of personal growth.

GO! Practice #4: Intentional Investing: How to Move to the Impacting Level

Moving to the Impacting Level of personal growth doesn't happen by accident. It requires the GO! Practice of *intentional investing*. **Intentional investing is the process of inspiring growth in others by making meaningful deposits in their personal growth.** These deposits help others experience their own personal growth revolution as they grow toward their missional potential. Intentional investing means taking full responsibility for the influence you have with others by using it for *their* good. There are six deposits that you can make in others to ensure your growth doesn't die with you.

> 1. Inspirational Modeling
>
> 2. Equipping Relationships
>
> 3. Growth Opportunities
>
> 4. Selfless Talent
>
> 5. Resource Allocation
>
> 6. Connection Capital

INSPIRATIONAL MODELING

Some personal growth is so obvious that people can't help but take a second look. When Jared Fogle lost 245 pounds, people noticed. In fact, it was hard *not* to notice. This kind of discipline is extremely inspirational. When people model drastic changes in behavior that lead to enormous personal transformation, you can't help but feel challenged by what they've done. And so the first deposit you can make to intentionally invest in others is to model inspirational behavior...on purpose.

I realize that not all personal growth is as visible as Jared's significant weight loss. Many times our growth doesn't offer inspiration until people get to know us, become acquainted with our story, or realize the price we've paid to grow. Regardless of how visible your growth is or is not, it doesn't change what sits in the driver's seat of all inspirational modeling—core values. Your values drive your be-

> Your values drive your behaviors and your behaviors reveal your values.

haviors and your behaviors reveal your values.

Your core values are the handful of non-negotiable, constant beliefs and priorities that guide your personal behavior. When you're clear about your values, you can make the important adjustments in your behavior to ensure how you live is aligned with what you believe. Values without aligned behavior are nothing more than *perceived* values. A perceived value is when you say that you value something because it's the *right* thing to say—but then your behavior doesn't back it up. An *actual* value, on the other hand, is something that's backed up by the full force of your behavior. In other words, what you say you value and how you actually behave match.

Inspirational modeling only takes place when your values and behaviors line up. As people watch you, interact with you, and follow you, they're increasingly inspired to grow because of the behavior you model. This is more than the tenacious application of the Living Level. It's choosing to *consistently* model the right behaviors and then challenging others to do the same. When you model inspirational behavior, it gives you the moral authority to invite others to join you in the journey of growth. Why is it that Frank Ross and Jared Fogle can speak with authority into others' lives? Because their authority is grounded in their inspirational behavior. When they speak or mentor, people listen, and then act.

The idea of core values can sound kind of scary. In fact, when you ask most people what their core values are, they look at you like you're from Mars. If you're not sure what your core values are—or if your values feel vague and incomplete—use the following fill-in-the-blank statement to uncover your *actual values:*

$$\left[\text{ I \underline{\hspace{3cm}} because I value \underline{\hspace{3cm}}.} \right]$$

The first blank represents a specific practice or behavior. It's what you do or how you act. The second blank represents the value that's driving whatever you wrote in the first blank. For example, you might say:

- "I <u>practice spiritual disciplines</u> because I value <u>my relationship with God</u>."
- "I <u>keep my work schedule in check</u> because I value <u>time with my family</u>."
- "I <u>always tell the truth</u> because I value <u>integrity</u>."
- "I <u>lead a small group</u> because I value <u>relationships</u>."
- "I <u>volunteer at the homeless shelter</u> because I value <u>the poor</u>."
- "I <u>give regularly to charities</u> because I value <u>generosity</u>."
- "I <u>workout consistently</u> because I value <u>my health</u>."
- "I <u>am an avid reader</u> because I value <u>personal growth</u>."
- "I <u>do things with quality</u> because I value <u>excellence</u>."

To identify your *actual values*, start by looking at your *actual behaviors*. Your most common behaviors will tell you what you value the most. To put it simply: how you spend your time and money tells you what you value. If what you see in your behaviors and practices isn't very inspirational, then identify your desired values and determine what behaviors need to change in your life. Again, if behaviors aren't aligned with values, then your values are nothing more than perceptions of a reality that doesn't exist.

EQUIPPING RELATIONSHIPS

One of the most powerful, yet most underestimated, ways to invest growth deposits in others is through *equipping relationships.* Equipping relationships are any kind of growth-focused relationship such as coaching, mentoring, discipling, or small groups. These relationships help people close their capacity gaps by equipping them with the knowledge and skills they need to maximize their missional potential. In the same way that equipping relationships were likely an essential part of your personal growth, you can also *be* an equipper for others.

Take coaching for example. Before you completely check out and dismiss yourself as "non-coach material" let me explain. In chapter four I described a coach as someone who provides assessment, insight, and motivation. Now think about those three things as they relate to one of your close friendships.

Have you ever helped a friend gain perspective by asking them a few clarity-boosting questions—questions that helped them cut through the fog surrounding their situation and think more clearly? If so, you've provided assessment. After listening and helping them gain some perspective, did you ask your friend a few more questions that helped them come up with a solution to their problem or even led to an "aha" moment in their life? If so, then you've stimulated insight. And when things got tough for your friend, did you come along side them with an encouraging word that affirmed your belief in them? If so, then you've provided motivation. Essentially, you took A.I.M. at their potential and carried out the three functions of a coach: Assessment, Insight, and Motivation.

So why couldn't you do that same thing for people around you who want to grow and need your help? That doesn't mean you're the "expert" life coach with the answers to all of life's problems. I like to coach people, but I'll also readily admit in which areas I have no business coaching people. I have the greatest coaching equity in my areas of strength...and so do you. Look for two or three areas in your life where you have passion and where you've honed your skills and acquired valuable experience. Then ask yourself, "How can I use this mix of strengths as a springboard to equip—or invest in—somebody else?"

When you're intentional about growing yourself and building trust with people, opportunities will emerge to equip others. It might be over lunch with a co-worker, in an annual review with an employee, in a small group with other Christ followers, or through a meaningful connection with your children. In a world where growth-focused encouragement is a rare commodity, most people are more than willing to receive some extra confidence-building support from somebody who cares. That's how it started with Frank Ross. Frank leveraged a young man's interest in ceramics as an opportunity to equip him for life. He encouraged Bill and offered valuable insight during those "coaching sessions" behind the potter's wheel.

As you gain experience, why not make the role of an equipper part of your own Growth TRAC. Identify a book or two that will help you understand how to invest in people or equip them to succeed. You might even participate in a leadership workshop, or if you're really aggressive, look for a coaching certification program. Then, as you ratchet up your skills, seek out more intensive equipping relationship. For example:

- *Employees* – Meet once a month with a new employee to discuss sticking points, help them get adjusted, or to coach them in their new role.
- *Volunteers* – Meet with a volunteer (in the church or community) to help them refine their skills, learn their role, or assume greater responsibility.
- *New Followers of Christ* – Meet a new believer once a week for prayer, Bible study, and accountability.
- *Students* – Mentor a student in a new skill or help a college senior put together a resume.
- *Small Groups* – Form a small group—perhaps like Regi Campbell—and focus on personal growth in a shared area of interest.

Whatever the scenario, YOU can equip *somebody*...but only if you're *intentional* about it. So let's be intentional—*now.* Reflect on the three people you listed at the conclusion of the last chapter. Who from your list can you help grow this week? What does your first step look like? How can you initiate an equipping relationship with them? In what area does it make the most sense to equip them? You don't need a formal coaching agreement to help somebody grow (unless of course you're offering formal coaching), but it does have to be deliberate. If you want to inspire growth in others, it requires meaningful, intentional, on-purpose deposits.

GROWTH OPPORTUNITIES

Over the years I've had several young leaders participate in ministry internships. One of the difficulties interns encounter is the imbalance of grunt work over growth work. While grunt work is a part of most internship programs, it usually drastically overshadows personal and professional growth and development. Don't get me wrong...I believe in the grunt work. It builds character and provides opportunity for young leaders to demonstrate faithfulness. However, students serving as interns really don't care to become professional filers, coffee brewers, photocopiers, and "unplug the crap in the toilet" workers. They want—and need—real experience and stretching opportunities that will bolster their future dreams.

The same is true for family members, friends, volunteers, colleagues, administrative assistants, and core members of your team. Each of them needs meaningful growth opportunities that are relevant to their situation...and you can provide those opportunities. Why not invite the people around you to:

- Participate in important meetings
- Engage in strategic planning sessions
- Research a project
- Attend a conference, seminar, or retreat
- Volunteer for ministry experiences
- Lead a task that adds value to the company
- Assume responsibilities that stretch their abilities and skills
- Co-lead a small group
- Organize a community service project
- Assist you in the classroom
- Shadow you on the job

A good way to keep "growth opportunities" in focus is to adopt a partner approach to some of your own growth goals. For example, if you're attending a conference, invite somebody to tag along. If you're reading a book on marriage or parenting, form a small group and discuss it together. If you're exercising, find a friend to go with you. If you're volunteering with a non-profit in your community, invite someone with a similar passion to serve with you. Not only will the partnership with somebody else help you stay on task, but it will give you a chance to invest in him too. The old saying, "Never do ministry alone" is at the crux of growth opportunities. What growth opportunities do you have on the horizon? Who will you invite to join you in that growth experience?

SELFLESS TALENT

You are gifted by God...but your gifts don't belong to you. You're simply a manager of the abilities, skills, and spiritual gifts that make up your God-given talent pool. Managers simply take care of what belongs to the owner. Since God owns your talent, that makes you the manager, or what the Bible calls "a servant" (Matthew 25:14-30). Servants always manage resources with the owner's best interests in mind—that's the essence of a *faithful* servant. Managers always ask themselves, "How would the owner want me to manage what he has entrusted to me?"

When you become a manager, it completely changes how you view and use the talents God gave you. Talent managers wear

> *Talent managers wear "servant lenses" which help them avoid three skewed perspectives on talent: insignificance, irrelevance, and inwardly-focused.*

"servant lenses" which help them avoid three skewed perspectives on talent: insignificance, irrelevance, and inwardly-focused.

People who view their talent as *insignificant* believe they have no talent, or that the talent they do have is insignificant compared to the "truly gifted." As a result, they never use their talent to invest in others because they don't think it will make any difference. These individuals don't see themselves as managers...they see themselves as unemployable.

Then there are those who see their talent as *irrelevant*. They view their talent strictly through the lens of their current job or responsibilities. For example, an auto mechanic sees relevance to his ability to fix cars when he's spending his days under the hood at work. But when it's time to clock out, his talent gets left on the shop shelf where it awaits his return the next morning. When people awaken to the reality that their gifts and abilities have relevance in more than one setting, they'll use those gifts to invest in others. It's like the mechanics at Willow Creek Community Church, outside of Chicago, who use their talents in the "CARS Ministry." These faithful volunteers put their skills to work by fixing cars that are given away to single moms and needy families. They're being selfless with their talent (the area where they've grown the most) so that they can bless somebody in need.

Finally, some people see their talent with an *inward focus*— their talent serves themselves, and nobody else. Unless they're getting paid or receiving special perks and privileges, these individuals keep their talent under lock and key. They see themselves as talent owners instead of talent managers.

Each of these perspectives—insignificance, irrelevance, and inwardly-focused—are ultimately selfish. People operating from these skewed perspectives view their talent with a low self-esteem, shortsightedness, or greed. Managers—or servants—recognize that talent has a much higher purpose: to glorify God and benefit others.

When Frank Ross selflessly shared his artistic talent with Bill Strickland, he did more than help a struggling teenager pick up a hobby. That selfless investment was the growth deposit that unlocked Bill's potential. Had Ross not made that investment, how many thousands of students and adults would have never been exposed to Manchester Bidwell Corporation's programs?

Each year when Regi Campbell invests his wisdom into eight young executives, he's doing more than building a professional network. He's helping a small group of men become the husbands, fathers, and Christian leaders God called them to be.

The key to depositing selfless talent lies in its two-fold application. First, you want to use your talent to bless others. And second, you want to strategically use your talent to help people grow. In the example of the CARS ministry, a mechanic is blessing a single mom when he fixes her car. If that same mechanic selflessly used his talent to mentor a student in auto mechanics, he would be helping somebody grow. The first application is about selfless giving. The second application is about selfless growing. Who are you serving with your talent?

RESOURCE ALLOCATION

I believe generosity is one of the most important character traits. Failure to cultivate a spirit of generosity always short-circuits the Impacting Level of personal growth. Growth is not cheap. It requires time, energy, focus, and yes, money. If you intentionally allocate resources to help others grow, you will help their dreams come true.

Recently, I was having breakfast with a friend when he told me about his teenage son's desire to join a summertime hiking adventure in Colorado. It was a great opportunity for spiritual and personal growth. As we discussed the details, he told me the adventure cost $3,000 and that his son was looking for thirty people to sponsor him $100 each. My friend wasn't asking me for money, but as soon as I heard about his son's interest in this growth experience, I knew I wanted to help. We signed up, wrote the check, and partnered with others to make his growth experience possible.

Don't be fooled into thinking that resource allocation means you have to be wealthy. Something as simple as buying a book, paying for a conference registration, or sponsoring a partial scholarship are perfect examples of using your resources to make growth possible for someone else. Jesus said, "From everyone who has been given much, much will be demanded; and from the one who has been entrusted with much, much more will be asked."[62] How are you using the blessings God gave you—regardless of their size—to bless and invest in others?

CONNECTION CAPITAL

Everybody is connected to somebody—usually lots of somebodys. Those somebodys comprise your network of relationships: friends, family members, work associates, vendors, pastors, community leaders, business owners, and schoolmates, just to name a few. Good relational networks reflect a lifetime of wisdom, valuable experience, and practical skills.

Your network of relationships is the backbone of your connection capital—the sixth and final growth deposit. Connection capital represents the size,

> *Connection capital represents the size, variety, depth, and authority of your relationships.*

variety, depth, and authority of your relationships.

- *Size* – Your relational network is a specific size...that is you have connections with a certain number of people.
- *Variety* – Your network of relationships includes different types of relationships representing different areas of expertise or experience.
- *Depth* – These relationships exist at varying levels of connection—some are deeper, closer relationships while others are more like surface level acquaintances.
- *Authority* – With each of your relationships, you have a certain level of authority (or influence). Your authority varies based on how deeply somebody respects you and how much they value your opinions.

So how is *connection capital* an intentional investing strategy? It's like a bridge. On one side of the bridge is the person you want to help grow. On the other side of the bridge is the individual—from your network of relationships—who can help them grow the most. You're nothing more than the bridge—the point of connection between the two. In other words, you're using your connections with others to make growth possible for someone else.

Author, professor, and leadership mentor Bobby Clinton observes that one of the functions of a mentor is to be a *sponsor*. He writes that a sponsor offers "protective guidance and linking to resources so that a leader reaches potential."[63]

Clinton asserts that the mentor sponsor acts as a door opener—an important function for helping people gain the opportunities and experiences necessary to fulfill their destiny. Here's the bottom line: as a sponsor, you're a connector—a matchmaker of the right mentor with the right mentee.

Frank Ross was a matchmaker when he intentionally used his connection capital to open doors for Bill Strickland. In his book, *Make the Impossible Possible*, Strickland captures the essence of Frank's connection capital and how it benefited his art pursuits during his senior year of high school:

> One piece I made won a Gold Key Award for outstanding work by a student from the Pittsburgh schools. More astonishingly, thanks to the web of contacts Frank helped me to establish in the local art world, I was asked to appear as a demonstrating artist at the Three Rivers Arts Festival, Pittsburgh's largest public celebration of the arts.[64]

What did Mr. Ross do for Bill? He loaned him his connection capital by connecting Bill with the people in his relational network that could open new growth opportunities for him.

Recently I had a similar growth experience when a respected author and leadership expert spoke to a group of church leaders. I was eager to spend time with this particular speaker because of his wisdom and organizational experience. His schedule was tight, as was his arrival and departure time. So I asked the host pastor if I could take this leadership authority to the airport at the conclusion of the event. He said, "yes," ultimately lending me his connection capital for a 30-minute intensive coaching drive to the airport. The last thing I wanted to do was waste this trip talking about the weather, so I prepared four questions to ask him.

When it was time to take him to the airport, we jumped in the car and I spent 60 seconds thanking him for coming and expressing my appreciation for the words he shared. Then I made the leap—"I have four questions I'd love to ask you," I said. Without skipping a beat, he said, "Shoot!" For the next 30 minutes I fired off my four questions—which in reality turned into 10 or 15 by the time you add in the follow-up questions. But that 30-minute drive was priceless. It was exactly what I needed to gain clarity in four important areas. And none of it would have been possible had the host pastor not used his connection capital to open a door—or to sponsor me—into that opportunity.

Here's a quick exercise that will help you maximize your connection capital. Pull out a sheet of paper and create two columns. In the left column make a list of your closest and most valuable relationships. Next to their names, in parenthesis, write a one-word description of the area in which they can best help someone grow. For example:

- Bill Smith (Business)
- Janet Baker (Prayer)
- Debora Keller (Parenting)
- Jason Carson (Exercise)

In the column to the right, list the three names you identified at the conclusion of the last chapter. Feel free to expand your list with other names too. In fact, because all of these people represent your network of relationships, you might choose to . list some of them in both columns. Now, next to the names in your second list, write one word or one phrase that represents this individual's greatest needs or dreams. For example:

- Erica Sanders (Cultivating spiritual disciplines)
- Tony Barclay (Launching a new business)
- Blake Packer (Marriage struggles)
- Sara Patterson (Creating a resume)

Once your two columns are complete, draw lines between the individuals in the left column that can best meet the needs or encourage the dreams of people in the right column. In the example above, Bill Smith might be able to help Tony Barclay with the launch of his new business. And Janet Baker could be the perfect match for Erica Sanders to cultivate the spiritual discipline of prayer. Look for these "matches" in your own network of relationships. Then, pick two or three and connect them with one another. Because you don't personally have (and never will have) everything that everyone in your relational network needs to grow, it's essential that you lean on your connection capital for help. That simple, yet very strategic, step will exponentially expand your ability to invest in others' growth.

From Intentional Investing to Others' Growth

Intentional investing is the GO! PRACTICE of the Impacting Level of personal growth. It's the discipline of using inspirational modeling, equipping relationships, growth opportunities, selfless talent, resource allocation, and connection capital to help others reach their potential. The OUTCOME of this practice is *others' growth.*

I want to challenge you to draw on all six deposits to invest in the people around you. Some will be more natural than others, but work hard to leverage each deposit for maximum impact. Remember, you don't want to take your growth with you to your grave. You want it to live on for many years—perhaps even many generations—after you're gone. You want your growth to inspire a growth revolution in the people you influence. The only way that will happen is if you are *intentional* about your *investing*. You must be deliberate.

Intentionality determines the size of your impact. Jared Fogle's intentional weight loss gave him the opportunity to intentionally invest in people who have struggled for years with their weight. Undoubtedly, these individuals are now investing in their own circles of influence. Frank Ross was also intentional—first about his own growth and then about his investment in Bill Strickland. Now, the deposits he made in Bill's life are creating change in the inner city. Intentionality isn't some kind of random winning lottery ticket. Intentionality is a day-by-day, week-by-week, and month-by-month deliberate effort to use the six growth deposits to add value to the people around you.

Your intentionality must increase as you climb the five levels of personal growth. In fact, at the Impacting Level, intentionality takes a sharp turn up and to the right. While none of the growth levels are automatic, the Impacting Level requires a special marriage between responsibility for your own growth and intentionality about others' growth.

What's amazing about intentional investing is that when you use your influence to help people grow, you often gain more influence in return. In the same way invested money compounds, invested influence compounds, too. I've seen this pattern repeated time and again in my own life. Even though my goal isn't to increase my influence, it's the natural by-product of investing in people.

The same is true for the people you're helping grow. Your investment in them is reaping increased influence. If you manage that influence with humility, God will use you to impact more people. If you manipulate that influence for your own personal gain, you'll lose it...as you should.

The College Professor Syndrome

In the early years of my college experience, I was increasingly frustrated by some of my professors' lack of experience. I'm sure I unfairly judged some of them at the time, but I couldn't shake the feeling that I was learning outdated ideas from inexperienced teachers. Over time, I've come to realize that some (certainly not all) college professors suffer from a syndrome characterized by skipping the Living Level and jumping straight to the Impacting Level.

This unfortunate practice embraces years of disciplined learning and thinking in preparation to impact young minds. But between learning/thinking and impacting is a giant non-negotiable ingredient called "done it."

When college professors attempt to teach what they've never done—or did so long ago that it's no longer relevant—they discredit their teaching. I realize there are exceptions to this generalization, such as extensive empirical research-based teaching, but for the most part, attempting to impact others without first living what you teach is like telling couples how to have a successful marriage when you've never been married.

Now, before you highlight this page in bright yellow marker and mail it to your former professors demanding a full refund, let me say clearly that I am pro-college, pro-education, and pro-qualified professors. I believe you should get as much education as you can, and I believe there are many professors who offer extraordinary insight and experience in their fields of expertise.

So what's my point? You can't skip the Living Level to get to the Impacting Level. It's your tenacious application resulting in personal transformation that gives you the authority to impact others. That doesn't mean you have to wait a lifetime before you can impact the people around you. Nor does it mean that you have to be an expert before you can intentionally invest in others. If that were the case, we would all be sunk. It simply means that the areas where you'll have the greatest impact are directly tied to the areas where you've personally *lived* what you've *learned.*

> You can't skip the Living Level to get to the Impacting Level. It's your tenacious application resulting in personal transformation that gives you the authority to impact others.

It is also worth noting that you will not move to the Impacting Level in every area of your life. In fact, (get ready to breathe a sigh of relief), you won't even make it to the Learning Level in some areas of your life. It's simply impossible to impact everybody in every area, and therefore your learning is usually limited to some key areas of your life. At the most, you'll experience the Impacting Level in a handful of areas—maybe less than half a dozen (if that).

Avoid i3 Thinking

On the opposite end of the "College Professor Syndrome" is "i3 Thinking—inferiority, inadequacy, and insecurity." i3 Thinking flourishes between the Living Level and the Impacting Level where mental barriers and the lies we tell ourselves abound. Dealing forcefully with i3 Thinking is crucial because it's the number one cause of taking all your personal growth with you to the grave.

Inferiority sells us a lie that everybody is better than us. Because the Impacting Level is all about helping others, it's really easy to identify somebody else that's more qualified. We say to ourselves, "If I had more money, more connections, or more talent, I would gladly invest in others." Then we point at someone we consider superior to ourselves and say, "Pick her!" Thoughts of inferiority trick us into thinking that we have to be at the top of our game before we can make a single deposit in somebody else's growth.

We don't want to succumb to the "College Professor Syndrome" so we swing to the other extreme and benchmark ourselves against "the most qualified." Inferiority makes the measure of success feel much higher than it actually is. We look at people like Mother Teresa and say, "Now, that was a saint! If I was like her, then I could impact others too." But how quickly we forget Mother Teresa's words: "If you can't feed a hundred people, then feed just one." Inferiority focuses on everybody else's superiority rather than on our personal responsibility.

A first cousin to inferiority is *inadequacy*. While inferiority makes the measure of success too high, inadequacy makes the assessment of one's self too low. Inferiority says, "They're too good for me." Inadequacy says, "I'm too bad for them." Rather than focusing on the handful of strengths—maybe even a single strength—that can contribute to others' growth, we lose perspective. What feels like a mountain of weaknesses dominates our focus. We tell ourselves lies, like "I don't have what it takes to coach someone," "My resource pool is too shallow to allocate anything meaningful to somebody else's growth," or "My network of relationships wouldn't mean a hill of beans to anyone else." While inferiority focuses on everybody else's superiority, inadequacy focuses on my insufficiency.

The third thinking barrier is driven by an attitude of fear. *Insecurity* focuses on the what-ifs and the what-might's. It produces anxiety and self-doubt about our ability to actually make a difference in someone's life. Excuses, like "What if I fail?" or "What if I look foolish?" or "What if I let someone down?" are promoted to CEO (Chief Execution Officer) in our minds. The truth is, you can "what if" yourself to death. Rather than focusing on the possibilities to impact others, insecurity focuses on the negative impact our efforts *might* have on us.

Mark Twain once said, "Keep away from people who try to belittle your ambitions. Small people always do that, but the really great make you feel that you, too, can become great."[65] Twain's words provide good perspective when i3 Thinking tries to undermine your impacting efforts. His words help you remember that you have something great to offer—and that you can inspire greatness in others.

As you embrace the GO! Practice of *intentional investing* by using the six growth deposits, be sure to avoid common pitfalls like the "College Professor Syndrome" and "i3 Thinking." As you do, you'll enrich your friendships, your family life will deepen, your professional contribution will accelerate, your cultural impact will grow, and you'll increasingly evolve into an "iron sharpens iron"[66] type of person. Before you know it, you'll inspire a personal growth revolution in somebody else. Such an impact is a gift that keeps on giving. When you are responsible and intentional with your influence, the day will come when you'll knock on the door of the final growth level...*Multiplying.*

GO! Starting a Personal Growth Revolution				
GO! Practice	Activates	Level of Personal Growth	Which results in	Outcome
Growth TRACing	⟶	The Learning Level	⟶	Growth Traction
Reflective Thinking	⟶	The Thinking Level	⟶	Mental Maturity
Tenacious Application	⟶	The Living Level	⟶	Personal Transformation
Intentional Investing	⟶	The Impacting Level	⟶	Others' Growth

Chapter 11

The Multiplying Level:
Exponential Growth

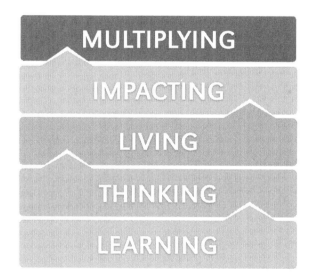

MULTIPLYING

IMPACTING

LIVING

THINKING

LEARNING

S everal years ago I traveled on three separate occasions
to Japan where I conducted a series of training experiences for students from American military bases. The
focus of the training was leadership, personal growth, and
how to discover your life purpose. At the conclusion of each

trip, I gave the students an assignment to create a customized growth plan similar to the Growth TRAC model I shared in chapter four. It was a practical step that helped students leave each experience with a roadmap for their personal growth. But this simple exercise actually did much more than that.

With each trip, I developed a growing friendship with Buddy Rathmell, my ministry contact in Japan. Buddy has a passion for leadership, so he took advantage of our time together to ask me every question imaginable. While we talked about a ton of ideas, my most important challenge to Buddy was this: "Be *intentional* about growing yourself and growing others." I encouraged him to create his own growth plan and to strategically invest in his students and leaders. Buddy took my challenge to heart. Just how much, I didn't know until I received an email from Buddy asking me to check out a blog post from Kate, one of his employees. Kate wrote:

I love this job, not only the ministry side or the admin side but also the fact that personal growth is encouraged, kept accountable, and practically considered part of my job description. Working for Buddy has been so encouraging, as he loves to read and leads us in such a way that we are strengthened and encouraged to figure out how the Lord can use us.[67]

Buddy concluded his email to me with these words: "Thanks for your impact on my life as you challenged me more than anyone else towards personal growth—so Kate owes a lot of that thanks to you." I've never met Kate but I've had the humbling opportunity to help her grow. How? By reaching the Multiplying Level of personal growth with Buddy. I personally grew, turned that growth outward by impacting Buddy, who then reproduced that growth in Kate. There's nothing more invigorating about lifelong learning than seeing your growth multiplied through others.

A Biblical Snapshot of the Multiplying Level

The concept of multiplication isn't new, especially in the world of leadership. While it may not happen as often as it should, most leaders understand that unless they move beyond the addition of workers to the multiplication of leaders, they will never maximize their potential, or the potential of the organization, ministry, or department they lead.

The same principle holds true with personal growth. You can grow yourself and even impact others, but multiplication is an entirely different level. In the same way a rock tossed in a pond creates a series of ripples, the Multiplying Level initiates an *enduring process of personal growth ripples.* Those ripples form when you help somebody grow, and then they turn around and invest in the growth of others. At this level, personal growth revolutions spread and even have the potential to go viral.

My grandmother—Violet Morley—recently passed away at the age of 92. She wasn't popular or famous or rich. You won't find her name in the history books of earth. But you can be sure that her name is remembered in the halls of eternity. She was a deeply spiritual woman with an unwavering commitment to prayer.

I'm convinced that Grandma's name was known in heaven *and* in hell—heaven because she spoke to Jesus daily, and hell because she fought the enemy fearlessly. She once told me,

"We have to do many different things, but *prayer* is the main thing."

On the day that she died, my mom told me that grandma's life was like a ripple—an enduring set of *prayer ripples*. Those ripples were felt in countless lives as one friend and family member after another surrendered their lives to Christ. At her funeral, letters were read and messages were shared by people who grandma "prayed into the Kingdom." On three separate occasions, those in attendance stood to their feet in applause of this tiny, insignificant lady who had a Mount Everest sized prayer life.

When I reflect on her prayer journey, I realize that she didn't take the journey alone. She mentored others in prayer, and she passed her prayer habit on to future generations. Prayer was more than a personal habit. It was a *multiplied* habit. She might have been a little lady, but she grew and multiplied a contagious prayer life...in her, around her, and beyond her.

A great biblical example of the highest level of growth is found in the book of 1 Thessalonians. Paul, Silas, and Timothy express gratefulness in their letter to the church in the city of Thessalonica. After an initial greeting, they write:

For we know, brothers loved by God, that He has chosen you, because our gospel came to you not simply with words, but also with power, with the Holy Spirit and with deep conviction. You know how we lived among you for your sake. You became imitators of us and of the Lord; in spite of severe suffering, you welcomed the message with the joy given by the Holy Spirit. And so you became a model to all the believers in Macedonia and Achaia. The Lord's message rang out from you not only in Macedonia and Achaia—your faith in God has become known everywhere.[68]

I want you to see the personal growth ripples in this passage. It started with Paul, Silas, and Timothy when they said, "You know how we lived among you for your sake." They began by *living* their growth. What they learned and thought transformed how they lived. Out of the overflow of personal transformation, they intentionally *impacted* the Thessalonians—"You became imitators of us and of the Lord..."

But the growth didn't stop there. The Multiplication Level kicked in: "And so you became a model to all the believers in Macedonia and Achaia. The Lord's message rang out from you not only in Macedonia and Achaia—your faith in God has become known everywhere." The following diagram illustrates it best.

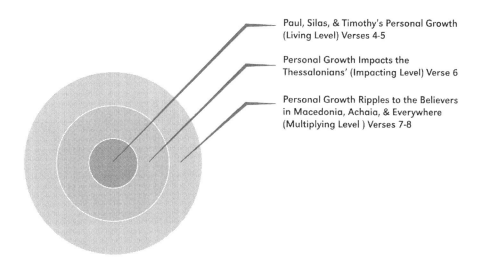

Paul, Silas, & Timothy's Personal Growth
(Living Level) Verses 4-5

Personal Growth Impacts the
Thessalonians' (Impacting Level) Verse 6

Personal Growth Ripples to the Believers
in Macedonia, Achaia, & Everywhere
(Multiplying Level) Verses 7-8

What the Thessalonians received from Paul, Silas, and Timothy's growth was more than an inspiring model that impacted how they lived. They were empowered to multiply that transforming work in the people around them. These men didn't keep their growth a secret. Nor did the Thessalonians let the growth ripple end with them. They *chose* to invest in the believers in Macedonia and Achaia who then, invested in people "everywhere." That's exponential growth. That's the power of multiplication. Paul, Silas, and Timothy's personal growth started a growth revolution in people they never even met.

The Biology of Growth

Your body has a mind-boggling 100 trillion cells in it. That means you have 14,000 times more cells in your body than there are people on the planet. And if you multiply 100 trillion by the 7 billion people on earth, that tells you how many *human* cells there are in the world (I'll save you the time and do the math for you...it's 7 with 23 zeros behind it). Billions of these cells wear out every day, but the multiplication process in your body keeps you alive. In fact, every seventy-two hours, the cellular lining of your stomach is replaced.[69]

So how do these cells multiply? It happens through the "cell cycle." The cell first grows until it reaches a size large enough to divide (otherwise the cell would just get smaller and smaller the more it multiplied). Then, the cell duplicates its DNA so that a copy exists for a second cell. Once the DNA is copied, the cell enters a checkpoint to make sure it's not flawed. Finally, the cell multiplies—a phase called mitosis—forming two cells with a set of the same DNA. Then the cycle begins again.

In his extensive research on the human body, cell biologist Bruce H. Lipton, Ph.D. conducted an experiment where he introduced toxins into a culture dish with human cells. Immediately the cells retreated away from the toxins, in a *protective* posture. In a separate culture dish, Dr. Lipton placed nutrients with the cells. These cells gravitated toward the nutrients in a *growth* posture.

Lipton observed: "These opposing movements define the two basic cellular responses to environmental stimuli. Gravitating to a life-sustaining signal, such as nutrients, characterizes a growth response; moving away from threatening signals, such as toxins, characterizes a protection response."[70] As humans, our survival mechanisms are categorized into these two primary functions: *growth* and *protection*.

These growth and protection mechanisms cannot operate simultaneously—that is, they cannot move forward and backward at the same time. In fact, growth is restricted in the human body when we move into a protective mode. Dr. Lipton uses an encounter with a mountain lion as an example. Your body would adopt a protective posture—allocating its energy to protection rather than growth—if you were standing face to face with a mountain lion, or any other form of danger, for that matter. That's a natural response. Like a gazelle spotted by a lion, your cells are screaming, "I don't want to be lunch... runnnnnnnnnnnnn!" And while God created your body with this protective mechanism, He didn't design you to live in a *constant* protection mode. You can't do "fight or flight" 24/7 without it taking a negative toll on your body.

Living in a constant protective mode hinders your ability to fight disease and think clearly, and limits your organs from carrying out their intended functions—the very thing that increases energy and produces growth. That protective posture takes energy...lots of energy. Lipton says, "A sustained protection response *inhibits the creation of life-sustaining energy.* The longer you stay in protection, the more you compromise your growth.

In fact, you can shut down growth processes so completely that it becomes a truism that you can be 'scared to death.'"[71]

Everything Multiplies or Dies

The five levels of personal growth are similar to the cell cycle in that *growth leads to multiplication.* However, your personal growth journey can come to a screeching halt if you live in the equivalent of a "protection mode." God designed you—in fact, called you—to multiply your growth, just like He designed the cells in your body to multiply. Scripture champions the value of multiplication in both the Old Testament (Moses, Jethro, and the children of Israel in Exodus 18) and in the New Testament (Paul, Silas, and Timothy in 1 Thessalonians 1).

When you choose *not* to multiply your personal growth, it's like retracting into protection mode. It's as if you're afraid of losing something valuable, like you're giving away a piece of wisdom that you'll never again retain. It's like stamping "No thanks!" on your ultimate growth potential. Growth without multiplication is like shaking your fist at the world and screaming, "My growth is mine, and nobody else can have it!" and then abandoning the very thing God created you to do...*multiply.* That sounds completely ridiculous. If your body did that, you'd be dead.

Oh how we fall prey to the myths of multiplication. We make it such an emotional issue—like a teenager on the drama/ trauma rollercoaster. I've seen it over and over in ministry. Take small groups for example. When pastors inspire small group leaders with a vision to train up new leaders and multiplying their groups, there's always a tinge of resistance. The complaints are all too common:

- "I don't want our group to multiply because we've become really great friends. Multiplying hurts too much."
- "Isn't multiplication about nothing more than numbers? I'm into quality not quantity."
- "Multiplication is too hard. Nobody in my group would ever lead their own group."
- "Is multiplication even biblical? Why would God want to break up biblical community?"
- "Multiplication is only meant for big groups. My group is the perfect size so there's no need for us to multiply."

What do all of these excuses have in common? They're myopic. That is, they're incredibly shortsighted! Every one of these excuses is *protecting what is* without giving any consideration to *what could be.* What if small group leaders looked at multiplication like this:

- "When I multiply my small group, I make room for people who are not connected...for people who have not yet experienced biblical community."
- "When I multiply my small group, I give opportunity for others to use their God-given gifts and abilities to serve."
- "When I make multiplication a priority, I become the most effective disciple-maker."
- "When I adopt the multiplication mindset, I'm adopting a biblical pattern for ministry."
- "When I multiply, I'm being unselfish."

Myopia doesn't just exist in small groups, it loves to root itself in personal growth too. In fact, shortsighted personal growth is actually the cause of myopia in so many other areas of life. If you're unwilling to empower other people to grow, then you're certainly not going multiply a small group, a local church, a business venture, or a global missions outreach. Sadly, the justification for myopic personal growth sounds all too common:

- "I don't want to multiply my growth because I'm not good enough. I'm not Moses or Paul, you know!"
- "Multiplication takes too long. I'm too busy to mess with it."
- "Isn't multiplication the pastor's job?"
- "I don't know how to multiply, so I guess I don't need to. God will understand."

How many times have you used one of these excuses to *not* help someone else grow? If you find yourself living comfortably in the land of myopia, you can't stay there any longer. *You've been living in protection mode long enough.* Your lease has expired. Everything was created to multiply—people, leaders, churches, small groups, and yes, *even your personal growth.* That's where the beauty is. When you move to the Multiplying Level, your personal growth lives forever. It gets passed from one person, to the next, to the next.

> When you move to the Multiplying Level, your personal growth lives forever.

Do you understand the implications of the Multiplying Level? When you choose *growth over protection*—in other words, when you choose *multiplication*—you pop the lid off of your life. You open yourself up to an unending world of possibilities. You experience the exponential power of personal growth. **You not only accelerate growth within you and around you, you accelerate growth BEYOND you.** So here's my question: why would you want your personal growth to die with you? At the Impacting Level others benefit from your growth. But at the Multiplying Level, others pass on your growth.

Characteristics of the Multiplying Level

The Multiplying Level is quickly lost in the personal growth process. The fact that it's the final level, and that few people really value it—much less maximize it—makes it easy to downplay its importance or uniqueness. However, personal growth wouldn't be complete without it. You know you're on the Multiplying Level when three characteristics are evident:

1. Others Internalize a Value for Personal Growth

2. You Show Others How to be Lifelong Learners

3. Growth is Passed On from One Person to the Next

OTHERS INTERNALIZE A VALUE FOR PERSONAL GROWTH

At the Impacting Level, others are shaped by your personal growth. But just because they've been shaped by your growth, doesn't mean they've embraced their own *value* for growth. They could simply be enjoying the benefits of your growth with no intention of putting in the effort to develop their full God-given potential.

This is a perfect example of the difference between *actual values* and *perceived values* that I addressed in the last chapter. Unless others are willing to internalize their own deep value for growth, they'll be confined to the playground of perceived values where they'll feel good about their intentions but won't get much accomplished.

Here's an important truth to take hold of: you cannot multiply what you do not possess. That's not rocket science, so let me take it one step further: just because you possess something does not mean you'll automatically multiply it. You can possess a value for personal growth, but you cannot force somebody else to adopt your values. There has to be an intrinsic desire within them to *want* to grow, even when they don't *want* to grow. You can intentionally invest in others and squarely challenge them to pursue personal growth, but at the end of the day, they make the choice whether or not to become lifelong learners and develop their full missional potential. Only when that challenge is *embraced*, *personalized,* and *internalized* has the value taken root.

So that raises a question: what can you do to pass your personal growth value on to others? First, *affirm the on-ramps.* Sometimes a personal growth value emerges when an individual encounters the on-ramps to personal growth (which I spoke of in chapter two). You know you're at the doorstep of the Multiplying Level when the people you influence embrace the learning attitudes of *humility* and *curiosity*, and are *resilient* during the difficult times of life.

While you can't force somebody to share your value for personal growth, you can affirm the on-ramps when you see them at work. In other words, compliment a person's curiosity by saying, "You seem really interested in (fill in the blank). You should look into that some more." Or if they exhibit humility, let them know how much you appreciate their teachable attitude. When they bounce back from a setback, tell them how much you admire their ability to turn difficult times into stepping-stones for growth. Your simple words of affirmation reinforce a growth value.

Second, *cultivate a growth environment.* While you can't *make* people grow, you can create an environment that fosters growth. It's like planting a tree. I can't make a tree grow, but I can kill it if I don't create the right environment for growth. The right environment means that I plant the tree in sunlight, water and fertilize it regularly, and prune it when necessary. The right environment provides the optimum place for growth to occur.

People are a lot like trees. You can't make them grow, but you *can* squelch any chance of growth if you haven't cultivated the right environment. If you want the people you interact with to embrace a value for personal growth, cultivate a growth environment by planting them in roles (or encouraging them to pursue roles) that will stretch them, adding water and fertilizer (like training and resources), and pruning (or coaching) them as they gain experience.

YOU SHOW OTHERS HOW TO BE LIFELONG LEARNERS

At the Impacting Level, you're intentional about helping people grow. But at the Multiplying Level, you take it one step further and help them become lifelong learners. What's the difference? The first is about making a single deposit in their growth. The second is about developing a lifelong habit of growth.

The second characteristic of the Multiplying Level is about more than teaching others *what* you've learned—it's teaching others *how* to grow. Author and mentoring expert Dr. Shirley

Peddy says, "A mentor's principal purpose is to help another develop the qualities he needs to attain his goals—without a mentor." That's the idea behind the Multiplying Level. You equip others to keep growing...*without you.* As long as others need you to grow, you can never reach the Multiplying Level. The old Irish saying captures it best: "You've got to do your own growing, no matter how tall your grandfather was."

> *"A mentor's principal purpose is to help another develop the qualities he needs to attain his goals—without a mentor."[72]*

So *how* do you teach people *how* to grow? Truthfully, there's not a silver-bullet strategy. The key is to identify a simple, replicable, yet customizable approach that works for you and the people you're helping. We'll go into more detail on how to show others how to become lifelong learners in the next chapter. The bottom line is, you must help the people you're impacting to take charge of their own growth. Then, once you've identified your strategy, share it with people through a coaching relationship, small group environment, or peer accountability relationship.

The key is to intentionally detach people from using you as their feeding tube. They must become self-feeders committed to their own growth and development. When that happens, you've given them a remarkable gift that will produce a lifetime of growth. For many, it will be the first time they pursue personal growth using a plan that somebody else—such as a parent, teacher, or employer—*didn't* create *for* them.

GROWTH IS PASSED ON FROM ONE PERSON TO THE NEXT

True multiplication happens when the ripple of your influence doesn't stop with the handful of people you're impacting. Just like the cells in your body, you duplicate the DNA of growth in someone else, who then multiplies the process over and over again. The Multiplying Level takes time because it's organic. You don't zap it in the microwave for 30 seconds and out pops another lifelong learner.

If growth ends with the person you've invested in, then you haven't reached the Multiplying Level. Only when they pass the growth on to somebody else have you multiplied. There's an aspect of multiplication that is literally out of your hands. But don't let that become your excuse for not multiplying your growth. As I mentioned earlier, the higher you go in the five levels of personal growth, the more intentionality it requires. At the Multiplying Level, you're working hard to help others take responsibility to turn their growth outward.

Multiplying a Personal Growth Revolution

When you reach the Multiplying Level of personal growth, something else begins to happen: the people you influence catch a vision for growth revolutions—for the five levels of personal growth. They understand the *inward* and the *outward* focus of growth. They're motivated to become lifelong learners on mission with God. That motivation translates into a personal growth approach that's unique to their God-given personality. As growth is pursued, it shapes their thinking, and, over time, personal transformation occurs as they live what they've learned.

You know by now that the Living Level is where most people call it quits, but you refuse to settle for mediocrity with the people you're influencing. So you keep nudging them and challenging them until they turn their growth outward, choosing to intentionally invest in others. And here's the most amazing part of this process: you likely won't even know most of the people they impact. Think about that! Your personal growth changes your life, the people you've invested in, and now people you don't even know. That's multiplication—*a true personal growth revolution!* It happened for Paul, Silas, and Timothy and it can happen for you too.

So what does it take to move beyond the addition of the Impacting Level (where you use your growth to ADD value *to* others) to the exponential power of the Multiplying Level (where you MULTIPLY your growth *through* others)? In the next chapter, we'll examine the final GO! Practice of the five levels of personal growth.

Chapter 12

Empowering People: How Far Can You See?

F rank Ross, the art teacher I introduced in chapter ten, was intentional about developing young Bill Strickland. Frank reached the Impacting Level of personal growth because he chose to turn his growth outward and mentor a young kid on the verge of dropping out of high school. However, the truth is, Frank didn't stop at the Impacting Level...he really reached the Multiplying Level. He not only impacted Bill Strickland, but he multiplied his impact through Bill to reach students like Sharif Bey.

Sharif was a shy, withdrawn student from Oliver High School who enrolled in the ceramics program at Manchester Craftsmen's Guild during his ninth grade year. Sharif didn't trust people easily and was generally suspicious of anyone who took an authentic interest in him. In his mind, there was always a catch...a bait and switch at the least. But regardless of how withdrawn Sharif was, his teachers believed in him and challenged him to pursue excellence. Soon Sharif's heart softened and he took his first stab at a lump of wet clay.

It didn't take long to realize that Sherif was a natural behind the potter's wheel. He started learning, growing, and experimenting with the clay, and he worked diligently to develop his own style. His passion grew, and for the first time in his life, he tasted sweet success. He was hooked! His confidence mushroomed and he started forging friendships with other students in the class.

During his senior year, Sharif received scholarship offers from several college art departments. He enrolled in Slippery Rock University, applied himself diligently, and earned a Bachelor of Arts. Most people in Sharif's situation would probably celebrate graduation and then take a mental vacation. After all, nobody would argue the success of an inner city kid beating the odds and graduating from college. Such a feat deserved a rest.

But Sharif's fire for personal growth was fully ignited. He wasn't going to douse it with the water of complacency or squelch it with the deceptive lure of educated arrogance. Instead, he viewed his graduation as a comma, and then finished the sentence with a Master's in Fine Arts and a PhD in arts education from Penn State.

Today, this shy kid—an unassuming and, some would say, uninterested teen from the ghetto—is the assistant professor of fine arts at Winston-Salem State University where he directs the arts education program. Reflecting on his time at MCG, Sherif Bey says, "Each success I enjoyed at the Manchester Craftsmen's Guild gave me reason to believe that more successes were possible. More than anything, it was that belief in my own potential that allowed me to build the life I lead today."[73]

How did Frank Ross reach the Multiplying Level of personal growth? Not only did he impact Bill Strickland, but he also empowered Bill to impact people like Sherif Bey. Today Bill is at the Multiplying Level as he empowers countless students and adults to become lifelong learners and pursue their full potential.

GO! Practice #5: Empowering People: How to Move to the Multiplying Level

The Multiplying Level unleashes potential on a grand scale. It's where personal growth becomes viral by leveraging the GO! Practice of *empowering people*. **Empowering people is a three-phase process:**

$$\left[\text{Challenging} > \text{Equipping} > \text{Releasing} \right]$$

CHALLENGING

Empowering people begins with a clear, uncompromising challenge from you to them. It's a challenge to embrace a lifelong learning habit. That's what Frank Ross and Bill Strickland have done. They elevated the expectations for students and challenged them to grow toward their full potential.

This challenge is inspiring and summons the depths of the soul and the convictions of the heart. It doesn't allow the people you're investing in to shirk the responsibility of personal growth, but instead places it squarely on their shoulders. Our culture has masterfully delegated personal growth to schools, companies, and churches. It's time for the people you impact to *own* their growth.

Let me make something very clear: when you fail to boldly challenge others to pursue lifelong growth, you rob them of their missional potential. That doesn't mean you can't pursue God's mission for your life without somebody looking you in the eyes and issuing a "you'd better get your butt in gear" challenge. But I have found, more times than not, that a bold challenge ignites the process. It's like the match that lights the fuse on the personal growth missile.

If you want to empower people, start by challenging them— unashamedly and unapologetically—to grow toward their God-inspired dreams and fulfill the mission God buried inside of them. This approach sheds a positive light on learning and helps others see personal growth as a dream-building tool rather than an order to "get your act together." Bold challenges arouse the sleeping giant of personal growth in the people you influence.

One final thought on the challenge to grow: personal challenges usually require personal relationships. It's difficult to challenge people to embrace a lifelong commitment to personal growth when you hardly know them. Do teachers and communicators make specific challenges like this to broad audiences? Yes! Are those challenges fruitful? They certainly can be. But everybody's not a teacher, professor, or motivational speaker. Most people work within a small network of relationships.

If you find yourself in this situation, cultivate closer connections with people until you earn the trust necessary to challenge them to grow. Sherif Bey didn't accept the challenge to grow to his full potential until he spent several days in the classroom.

He shares, "My teachers were telling me I was capable of more than I thought, and making it clear their expectations were very high. That was disorienting. I'd never had any context for interacting with people who treated me like that, or thought of their own lives that way."[74] But that constant encouragement and belief opened Sherif's mind to a whole new world. When somebody *knows that you care and believe in them*, you'll earn the credibility to challenge them to grow.

EQUIPPING

Empowering people doesn't end with a challenge. You must follow your challenge with a practical next step that makes your bold challenge achievable. In other words, you must equip others with a skill that will enable them to grow for the remainder of their lives.

In chapter four I shared the Growth TRAC as a practical tool to generate growth. When you help people learn the Growth TRAC skill (or some variation of it), you're teaching them *how* to become lifelong learners. It's like the old adage that says, "Give a man a fish and you'll feed him for a day. Teach a man to fish and you'll feed him for a lifetime."

You might argue that a Growth TRAC isn't necessary to grow...and I would agree with you. Growth isn't dependent on a neatly packaged formula or a memorable outline. The very fact that my growth-planning model spells "TRAC" annoys some of you. That's fine. I get it! And I'm okay with it. But here's what you do need to know if you're going to equip a friend to become a *lifelong learner*: **the best learning is self-directed.**

People are uncomfortable with one-size-fits-all growth programs. Each of us is unique and has different strengths, challenges, opportunities, schedules, dreams, and personality types—all of which influence how we learn. Author Reggie McNeal observes, "Today, people learn at their own speed, on their own time, at their own convenience. In this new arrangement, power is ultimately transferred to the information consumer. Learners get to craft their own learning path."

> "Today, people learn at their own speed, on their own time, at their own convenience. In this new arrangement, power is ultimately transferred to the information consumer. Learners get to craft their own learning path."[75]

Using some form of a Growth TRAC (or learning path) is a practical way to take advantage of self-directed learning. If you're going to reach the Multiplying Level of personal growth, you can't just spoon feed a person's growth to them. You've got to put the spoon in *their* hand so they can feed themselves. A Growth TRAC—or some variation of a growth strategy—is like a spoon that allows people to feed themselves.

I'm not naïve enough to believe that the personal growth model that I present in this book is the *only* way to grow on purpose. There are other strategies that will work just as well. You don't have to follow my "pathway" to be a lifelong learner. However, don't place the responsibility for your growth in the hands of your church, college, or company, either. And don't insist that people sign-up for your "program" because supposedly it's the best way to grow. People development, not program development, maximizes personal growth. Otherwise, you're doing nothing more than cramming square pegs (people) into round holes (programs).

So what does all of this have to do with the Multiplying Level of personal growth? After all, isn't the Growth TRAC and the need for lifelong learning just rehashing the Learning Level?

Here's why this is important: **it's easier to multiply some-thing when you have a reproducible, yet customizable, model that you can share with others.**

Now, I know what you're thinking: "But isn't a model noth-ing more than a round hole (a program)? And isn't that what you just told me *not* to force people into?" Look again at the statement I just made—"reproducible, YET CUSTOMIZABLE, model."

Think about it! If you were going to teach me how to play golf, how to lead a small group, or how to create a business plan, you would probably start with a proven model. That doesn't mean you wouldn't make your own tweaks to the model or even encourage me to customize the model to match my per-sonal style. God made us unique, so most of us don't fit neatly in someone else's model. At the same time, most of us *do* need a starting point—and that's what the model is...a place to start.

If you're going to inspire somebody to grow, don't leave them empty handed. Teach them *how* to grow by putting a proven growth tool—mine, yours, or someone else's—in their hands. With a growth-planning model, you're not signing people up for someone else's program. You're simply sharing a process to help people pursue customized, personalized, lifelong learn-ing that helps them reach *their* missional potential.

Although I'm biased toward the Growth TRAC, I'm not mar-ried to it. I'm married to *growth.* And I want you to be married to growth too. And I want you to help others be married to growth. So if you're going to reach the Multiplying Level, **you've got to make growth "marry-able"—that is, consistently attain-able for others—by giving them a tool that works.**

This tool—or skill—is the path to the pot of gold at the end of their personal potential rainbow. And when you show people how to grow, you just put that pot of gold in reach. Providing them with such a tool allows them to start their own personal growth revolution. The model or strategy that you choose is simply a starting point. What will you use to show others how to grow?

RELEASING

The final aspect of empowering people is releasing them to impact others. At some point you need to sit down with them and encourage them to move their growth beyond an internal discipline to an external focus. For most people, this isn't natural. It's much easier to focus all our attention on ourselves. But the Impacting and Multiplying Levels of personal growth are not self-centered. If you truly want to move beyond addition and begin multiplying your impact, you must inspire the people you've invested in to turn around and do the same for somebody else.

With such a charge comes a flood of emotions. Most people do not see themselves as a coach or as someone who can inspire others to grow. That's where, once again, you'll need to speak words of life into their untapped potential. Believe in them. Affirm them. Love them. Encourage them. But, above all, *release them* to go and help others grow.

The act of "releasing" is expressed in different ways at the Multiplying Level. For example, you can release people to multiply a *value* for personal growth. Here you empower people to do everything possible to help others adopt their own value for lifelong learning.

You can also release them to multiply specific attitudes, habits, and skills that you helped them learn. Once they've learned these new behaviors, encourage them to help somebody else grow in that same area.

Finally, you can release them to multiply the *how* of personal growth. As I described above, inspire people to show others *how* to grow by teaching them skills that produce lifelong learning habits.

For several years I've invested in the growth of a young leader named Jonathan. Upon the conclusion of an internship with me, Jonathan gave Karen and I a letter. After a kind introduction, he wrote:

> The amount of change and growth that has occurred in my life is a direct result from your love and ministry in my life. No words can express the amount of appreciation that I have for what you guys have done for me. There will be no ministry that I will be a part of later in life that will not have an imprint of you in it. Thank you for your belief in multiplication and belief in me.

I am humbled by the words Jonathan shared in his letter. I am grateful for the opportunity to invest in his life. But, more than anything, I am energized by the value he has gained for multiplication. Did I *challenge* him to grow? Yes! Have I *equipped* him to grow? Absolutely! But the empowering process didn't stop there. I *released* him to help others grow, too. Over the last year, Jonathan has started meeting with other young leaders and investing in their personal growth.

Taking the Journey to the Multiplying Level

So, practically speaking, what does the Multiplying Level look like? I've given you a couple of examples from my own life, as well from the lives of Bill Strickland and Frank Ross. But let me clearly illustrate the process.

Let's say, for example, you've personally grown a great deal in your relationship with Christ. You're not perfect by any stretch of the imagination, but you've cultivated three important habits: prayer, Bible reflection, and worship. These habits have created a welcoming environment for the transforming work of the Holy Spirit in your life. So how do you use your growth to inspire spiritual growth *in* others (at the Impacting Level) and *through* others (at the Multiplying Level)?

Your first step is to identify someone in your network of relationships who wants to grow in the same area that you have—in this case, a relationship with Christ. Let's say, with a bit of prayer and reflection, your mind is drawn to a co-worker—we'll call him Rich—who recently became a Christian.

You invite Rich to lunch, where, after some casual conversation, you gently guide the discussion toward faith. Rich's eyes light up as he talks about his new found relationship with God, as well as his uncertainty about what to do next. You see an open door, so you make the leap, saying, "Rich, I'm really excited to hear what God's doing in your life. That's awesome! And I'd love to help you grow in your relationship with God. Is there anything I can do to help?"

Rich isn't quite sure how to respond, so he mumbles something about not understanding the Bible or how to talk to God. You pipe up, "I know exactly how you feel. When I first committed my life to Christ, I felt like a kid in a candy store. I was so overwhelmed that I didn't know where to start."

Rich nods, acknowledging similar feelings. You add, "It wasn't until I found somebody to give me some guidance that I really started moving forward in my relationship with God." His interest piqued, Rich asks, "So what should I do?"

In response to that question, you make a simple, non-intrusive suggestion. "What if we met together for breakfast once every week or two to talk about how to grow our relationship with God? Do you think something like that would help?" Rich is curious at the thought, "*Our* relationship with God?"

"Sure!" you reply, "I'm not some theologian with all the answers, so I'd love to meet with you and we can learn together." Rich finds the idea to be exactly what he needs. He asks, "So what do I need to bring to the meeting?" Your response is simple, "Let me see if I can find something that would be a great discussion guide for us to work through together—something like a Bible study for new Christians. Why don't you bring your Bible and a pen...we'll start there." So you schedule your first breakfast meeting in two weeks.

With that simple interaction, you've set the stage to move to the Impacting Level with Rich. You check the local bookstore as well as a couple of online retailers for a great study for followers of Christ who are new in their faith. Once you find a study guide, you *allocate resources* to purchase two copies of the material and then spend a few days familiarizing yourself with the content. The more you prepare, the more excited you are about the possibilities. Your prayer is simple: "God, help me to help Rich."

Impacting Time

Over the next few weeks you engage Rich in an *equipping relationship* as you meet weekly over breakfast. Each time you get together, you study the curriculum and discuss what it means to follow Christ. You allow Rich to hear you pray simple prayers (nothing fancy or intimidating) and you even help Rich create his own prayer list.

As the journey deepens, you share with Rich a practice that you call "The 3 Rs: Read, Reflect, and Respond." It's a user-friendly strategy you learned several years ago to help you read a passage of Scripture, reflect on what it means, and respond with one simple act of obedience. In fact, you agree to begin your meetings with each of you sharing one Scripture passage you read the previous week, what it means to you, and how you're applying it to your life. Both of you are hearing the work God is doing in the other's life.

With every meeting, you see Rich's faith growing. Sometimes he asks you tough questions that you don't have answers to, but you commit to search the Scriptures and do your best to find answers. Occasionally, you even call your pastor for help. And in those times when you have to say, "Rich, I don't know the answer...and I don't know where to turn to find it," Rich appreciates your authenticity and transparency.

After three months of meeting together, you decide to deepen your intentional investment in Rich by inviting him to join you for a spiritual retreat with your church—a great *growth opportunity* for both of you. He agrees and the weekend turns out to be an incredible highlight in Rich's life as God begins healing some of his past hurts with his ex-wife. Wanting to take full advantage of the retreat, you leverage your *connection capital* to help Rich connect with some other men. In just two days, Rich feels like he's hit it off with a couple of other guys.

After the retreat is over, you continue investing in Rich. By now you've completed your original study guide, and it's time to up-the-ante. You know you can't spoon feed Rich forever, so you decide to help Rich create his own pathway for growth.

One day at breakfast, you share with Rich the words of Hebrews 6 where the writer challenges Christians to "leave the elementary teachings about Christ and go on to maturity." You say, "Rich, you've grown so much over the last few months, and I'm really proud of you. But today I'd like to share with you something that will help you grow for the rest of your life." Rich sits up with anticipation and leans forward, all ears.

You pull out a napkin and write T-R-A-C down the left side. You tell him, "Rich, if you're going to keep your faith alive and growing, you're going to need a unique plan that works just for you—kinda like a customized spiritual growth plan. We'll call it a spiritual Growth TRAC—spelled T-R-A-C."

Pointing your pen at your napkin, you say, "The 'T' stands for 'Target.' In other words, you start by pinpointing a specific growth goal." "Like, 'to be closer to God?'" Rich asks. "Good start, but let's be more specific." You remind Rich of a conversation a couple weeks ago when he expressed interest in learning more about the beatitudes. "What if your growth target was this: *'Study the beatitudes and identify one practical step to apply each beatitude to my life.'* That makes your target a bit easier to measure." "Makes sense," Rich declares. "I like it!"

Then you highlight the "R" for "Roadmap" and explain that reaching his target will take a roadmap...like it takes a roadmap to drive across the country. You talk briefly about one of your own growth goals and how you crafted a specific "roadmap" that leveraged training, resources, relationships, and experiences to help you reach your Target. This provides a practical example for Rich and helps him understand what a good roadmap looks like.

Together you brainstorm some practical steps Rich can take as a part of his roadmap to reach his target:

- Read the beatitudes in three different versions of Scripture
- Read a book on the beatitudes
- Listen to a podcast sermon series on the Beatitudes
- Create a journal to capture major takeaways from the beatitudes
- From the journal, identify one major application point for each beatitude

You wrap up the process by explaining that "A" is for "Accountability" and that "C" is for "Check-ups." To help drive these concepts home, once again you share a couple of examples from your own Growth TRAC.

With that, you give Rich a challenge to fine-tune his spiritual Growth TRAC before your next meeting. You tell him, "You want to be as specific as possible. Even with your roadmap, you'll want to identify the book you plan to read and the sermon series you want to listen to. The more specific your Growth TRAC is, the easier it will be to measure. And don't hesitate to call or email me if you get stumped. It's okay. Sometimes a Growth TRAC is really easy to create, and other times, depending on the focus, it takes a bit more effort."

The next week Rich comes to the meeting and shares his completed Growth TRAC with you. When he gets to the "Accountability" portion, to your surprise, he says, "I asked Bill, who I met at the church retreat, if he would be my accountability partner. We're going to get together once a month for lunch and he's going to ask me three questions:

- What are the major takeaways you've written in your journal to help you grow in your understanding of the beatitudes?
- What action steps have you identified to help you apply the beatitudes to your life?
- What progress have you made in applying the action steps?

You're ecstatic. Rich's entire Growth **TRAC** is well developed and he's learning *how* to grow without you having to spoon-feed him. You congratulate Rich, and then let him know that he can create a Growth **TRAC** for any area of his life— spiritually, mentally, relationally, and physically.

Rich raises his eyebrows, "You know, you're right. I could see this working on my job. I really need to improve my team-building skills. I could create a **TRAC** to help me get started. And I've been saying for over a year that I've got to get in better physical shape. I've set goals before, but now I realize my plan was flawed."

"What was missing in your plan?" you inquire. "Well," Rich says, "to begin with, I never thought about everything that could help me grow. Usually I picked one thing and left it at that. Now I realize that training and resources can make a big difference. And relationships! I never thought about asking someone to mentor me or be a workout partner."

"Anything else?" you ask. "Yeah! Accountability! I hate the tough questions but now I realize they're essential to my growth."

You continue to meet with Rich. In the weeks that follow you stay up to date on the implementation of his Growth TRAC and you challenge Rich to follow through on creating a Growth TRAC for his teambuilding goal and for his physical health.

You're also aware that prayer has been a big challenge for Rich, so you keep this in focus during your meetings. "Rich, even though you can't see God, He's right there with you and He's ready to hear from you each day. He's not only your God, He's your friend too. So talk to him like you and I are talking right now." At first it's slow, but when God answers Rich's prayer for a friend to find Christ, the tide begins to turn.

Multiplication Time

Another six months pass, and you recognize that Rich has reached a place where he needs to take his personal growth to another level. He's been learning...a lot, and as he has prac-ticed the "Three R's" (Read, Reflect, and Respond), you've seen his thinking mature. Perhaps most encouraging is that the areas where you've grown the most—worship, Bible study, and prayer—are being replicated in Rich. He still has a great deal to learn, but you know it's time for Rich to invest in some-body else.

One day over breakfast, you pull out a pen and draw the five levels of personal growth on a napkin. You begin to explain to Rich that he's been on a *learning, thinking,* and *living* journey for the last nine months in His relationship with Christ. You remind him of the mountaintop experiences he's had and point to the spiritual habits he's developed since you first started meeting.

Rich is encouraged and expresses his deep appreciation for the time you've spent meeting with him. But then you pique his curiosity with these words: "Rich, the best is yet to come." With that, you turn his attention to the Impacting and Multiplying Levels.

You begin to explain the importance of investing in people—just like you've invested in Rich. You explain the six growth deposits—inspirational modeling, equipping relationships, growth opportunities, selfless talent, resource allocation, and connection capital—and point to times when you've made these deposits in Rich's life.

Then you drop the bomb: "Rich, I think it's time for you move to the Impacting Level." Rich gets a bit nervous, "Uh, what do you mean?" With a serious, but gentle resolve, you look Rich straight in the eyes and say, "What I've been doing with you for the last nine months, I think you should do that for someone else...someone who's new in *their* faith."

At first Rich is uneasy with the idea as he explains how inadequate he is to "mentor" someone else when he still has so much to learn. But you gently remind him of all of the times you didn't have answers to Rich's questions and how you simply "learned together."

Then you tell him, "You have nine months more knowledge than someone who came to Christ yesterday." Rich knows you're right. So with a hint of trembling in his voice, he says, "So what do I need to do? Where do I start?" With that, you direct Rich's attention to his friend Brian who recently made a commitment to follow Christ. "You could do the same thing for Brian that I've done for you." Rich smiles, "I guess you're right."

Then you point your pen to the Multiplying Level on your napkin. "Rich, when you start investing in Brian, you'll be at the Impacting Level and I'll move to the Multiplying Level. And one day—maybe nine months from now—you'll have this same conversation with Brian. And then you'll move to the Multiply-ing Level too. Who knows? Maybe the day will come when you even multiply those other growth goals you created—team building and physical health."

Rich gets it. He takes your challenge to heart and that week he invites Brian to lunch. And the process begins again. You're helping Brian grow because you've multiplied your growth through Rich. He's impacting; you're multiplying. And if you've done your job with Rich, he'll multiply one day too, adding one more ripple to your growth.

That's how multiplying works. That's how personal growth revolutions begin. It's not some fancy recipe with a million layers of complication to wade through. It's all summed up in one really important word: INTENTIONAL. To multiply growth takes intentionality. It doesn't happen by accident.

Where Will You Multiply?

You can take the situation that I just described with Rich and apply it to any area of your life where you've exhibited growth. Whether you're growing spiritually, mentally, relationally, or physically, you can multiply that growth through others. Here are just a *few* areas where you might be able to multiply your growth:

Growth Multiplication Areas

• **Spiritual** – Prayer, Bible reading/study, worship, fasting, Scripture memorization, sharing your faith, character development, the fruit of the Spirit, the gifts of the Spirit, Biblical worldview

• **Mental** – Job skills, your area of expertise, leadership, finances, time management, communication skills, musical abilities, writing skills, sports, technology, business, science, math, languages, outdoors, arts, media, government, social justice, overcoming addictions, abuse recovery

• **Relational** – Marriage, parenting, people skills, social intelligence, emotional intelligence, friendships

• **Physical** – Health, fitness, nutrition

At the Multiplying Level, you not only impact people with what you've learned and applied to your life, but you challenge them to pass that growth on to someone else. That growth can be in ANY area, so don't limit your multiplication potential to one thing.

Here's your chance to get started. In the blank below, write the area of your life where you've grown the most. If there's more than one area, feel free to list them, too.

My Greatest Growth Area(s) Is:

_____

Now, how can you take that area of growth and begin multiplying it over and over? This is not something you do overnight. It starts by investing in others and then empowering them to do the same.

Growth Replication:
The Outcome of Empowering People

Empowering People is the GO! PRACTICE to the Multiply-ing Level of personal growth. It's the very intentional prac-tice of challenging, equipping, and releasing people to multiply growth in others and start a personal growth revolution. The OUTCOME of this practice is *Growth Replication.*

To replicate implies copying, duplicating, or reproducing. In other words, the attitudes and disciplines of personal growth are replicated—passed on from person to person—with an en-during impact wherever it reaches.

At the Multiplying Level, growth is like an endowment that continues to payout. Because of your initial investment in oth-ers' growth, combined with the empowering process, the rate and scope of your influence ac-celerates. It moves from direct to indirect as the people you've influenced begin to invest in others.

> At the Multiplying Level, growth is like an endowment that continues to payout. Be-cause of your initial investment in others' growth, combined with the empowering process, the rate and scope of your in-fluence accelerates.

Sustained impact takes place at the Multiplying Level. Eventually, your personal growth reaches a critical mass as the compounding affect of your growth influences people beyond your immediate reach. With no additional time invested, you are growing people you'll never meet.

Co-Dependent Growth

There's a specific temptation you will face before crossing into the Multiplying Level. It's the dark side of the Impacting Level and is born out of insecurity. *It's the need to feel needed.* This co-dependent growth attitude seduces many, and is the great chasm between impacting and multiplying.

Because investing in people is very rewarding, you'll experience great satisfaction in helping people reach their full missional potential. In fact, God may use you to help somebody find freedom from an addiction, develop their parenting abilities, learn a new skill, excel in their profession, exercise regularly, or experience the undeserved grace of God. With every "win" in the growth journey a subtle attitude of dependency will poke it's ugly head up, looking for a place to settle in your mind. If you're not careful, you'll convince yourself that the people you've invested in cannot survive, much less thrive, without you.

At some point people need to detach themselves from our feeding tube. That doesn't mean we can't continue to invest in their growth. It means that *we* are no longer their growth plan—we're simply *part* of it.

Dependence replaces empowerment when we think *for* others rather than releasing them to grow for themselves. How many times have you seen somebody insist on spoon-fed growth because they never put on the big-boy pants of personal responsibility? When we do not empower others with the skills to grow themselves and challenge them to intentionally invest in others, personal growth becomes an end in itself. Rather than using our growth to inspire the transformation of people, organizations, and cultures, we do nothing more than gather at the table of intellectual gluttony to impress one another with the size of our brains.

206 GO! Starting a Personal Growth Revolution

Don't Confuse Investing and Empowering

Insecurity doesn't plague everybody at the doorway to multi-plication. Many people find great inspiration in empowering others and experiencing growth replication. However, it's also easy to confuse investing at the Impacting Level as the activity of the Multiplying Level. When you're making intentional invest-ments in people, you can't assume those investments equate to the empowerment of others. They do not! The following is a contrast of the differences:

INVESTING	EMPOWERING
Makes a deposit in others' growth	Instills a personal growth value in others
Teaches others what you know	Teaches others how to grow
Focuses on the growth of others	Focuses on releasing others
Adds personal growth to others	Multiplies personal growth through others

Investing in others' growth is a great contribution—one that is essential to impacting people and making a difference in the world. But empowering people is investment to the one hundredth power. Rather than doing all the investing, you em-power others to invest with you, for you, and beyond you. The question is, *how far can you see?*

It's Your Turn to Climb the Five Levels of Personal Growth

Throughout this book you've learned about the characteristics of the five levels of personal growth. You've discovered the unique GO! Practice that puts each level in reach. And you're aware of the specific outcome that results with each level. The following chart provides a great overview.

GO! Starting a Personal Growth Revolution				
GO! Practice	Activates	Level of Personal Growth	Which results in	Outcome
Growth TRACing	⟶	The Learning Level	⟶	Growth Traction
Reflective Thinking	⟶	The Thinking Level	⟶	Mental Maturity
Tenacious Application	⟶	The Living Level	⟶	Personal Transformation
Intentional Investing	⟶	The Impacting Level	⟶	Others' Growth
Empowering People	⟶	The Multiplying Level	⟶	Growth Replication

Now it's your turn. Which level are you on in each area of your life? Regardless of where you find yourself, you can take a step forward. The choice is yours. Your missional potential is waiting for you...and so is the potential of the people you influence. Put on your climbing boots. Start a personal growth revolution in you and around you. It's your move. GO!

PART THREE

Appendixes

--- *Appendix A* ---

Growth Area Assessments

T he following is a list of assessments that will help you in the creation of your Growth TRAC. While this is not an exhaustive list, it's a good place to start for a handful of key areas of life. Each assessment will help you identify a starting point for growth and give you the context necessary to craft a Growth TRAC that enables you to move forward.

1.   **Spiritual Health Assessment –** Evaluate your spiritual health in five areas: worship, fellowship, discipleship, ministry, and evangelism. Learn more at www.smallgroups.net.
2.   **Wellbeing Finder™ –** The Wellbeing Finder™ was developed by Gallup and assesses your wellbeing in five areas: career, social, financial, physical, and community. The tool allows you to assess your wellbeing, track your wellbeing over time, discover patterns, and take action steps toward greater health. Learn more at www.wbfinder.com.
3.   **Strengthsfinder 2.0 –** Gallup's ground-breaking Strengthsfinder assessment helps you identify your top

five talent themes. Learn more at www.strengthsfinder. com.

4.   **MyPassionProfile** – The MyPassionProfile assessment helps you discover your passions so that you can leverage your strengths in your passion areas to live a fruitful and fulfilling life. Learn more at www.mypassionprofile.com.

5.   **Marriage Assessments** – Drs. Les and Leslie Parrott have developed several assessments to help you understand and improve your marriage. Some of their assessments include a pre-marital assessment, a L.O.V.E. Styles Profile, a Time Style Assessment, and more. Learn more at www.lesandleslie.com.

6.   **Leadership Practices Inventory** – This assessment is based on the research and writings of Jim Kouzes and Barry Posner (authors of *The Leadership Challenge*) and gauges proficiency in The Five Practices of Exemplary Leadership®. This tool is available as an individual assessment or a 360-degree observer-based tool. Learn more at www.lpionline.com.

7.   **Finishing Well Risk Factor Assessment** – This assessment provides insight into your areas of highest vulnerability and provides practical insight to help you finish well. Learn more at www.keepgrowinginc.com.

Using Your Personality Type to Create a Growth TRAC

xtensive research has been conducted on different per-
sonalities, which has deepened our understanding of
how people view and respond to life. While there are
numerous quality personality assessments on the market, I
want to focus on the Myers-Briggs Type Indicator (MBTI).

During the 1940s, Katharine Briggs and her daughter, Isa-
bel Briggs Myers, inspired by the research of Swiss psychia-
trist Carl Jung, created The Myers-Briggs Type Indicator. The
MBTI is a personality instrument that measures individual differences in four preference areas. As you read each of these
areas, consider which of them best describes you.

- *Extraversion/Introversion* – Extraversion/Introversion is focused on what energizes you. Extravert (E) types are primarily energized by interacting with people. They enjoy
  being with others and tend to be outgoing, expressive,
  and have a wider network of relationships. Introvert (I)
  types, on the other hand, are energized by being alone.

They are more reserved, reflective, and think before speaking. Again, these are simply preferences—they do not represent a right or wrong.

- *Sensing/Intuition* – Sensing/Intuition is a preference that shapes how we prefer to collect or gather information. It focuses on perception. Sensing (S) types perceive reality and are attuned to information gathered using the five senses—sight, sound, taste, touch, and smell. The Sensing type is detail oriented, specific, practical, and concrete. Intuition (N) types lean on their intuitiveness—somewhat of a gut instinct—to gather information. They are more theoretical, think of the possibilities, and are abstract.

- *Thinking/Feeling* – Thinking/Feeling is a preference that affects decision-making. Thinking (T) types are much more logical, analytical, and objective in their decision-making. Feeling (F) types, on the other hand, are much more sympathetic and subjective in their decision-making. They tend to demonstrate mercy where as Thinking types tend to be more impersonal.

- *Judging/Perceiving* – The Judging/Perceiving preference relates to your orientation toward the outer world. The Judging (J) types are more structured, decisive, and organized. They excel in getting things done and checking things off their to-do list. The Perceiving (P) types like options. They are much more spontaneous, flexible, and if they make a list, they'll likely lose it. The Judging types like to have a plan and the Perceiving types like to keep all their options open.

If you take the Myers-Briggs Type Indicator (which you can learn more about at www.myersbriggs.org), you will discover your unique personality type (made up of a combination of the preference areas described above). You might even have a general idea of what your personality is just from reading the brief descriptions. For example, you might be an ESTJ (Extraversion/Sensing/Thinking/Judging) or an INFP (Introversion/Intuition/Feeling/Perceiving). There are 16 different possible combinations. When you discover your combination, you'll learn a great deal about your personality.

Personalities and Your Growth **TRAC**

So what does all of this have to do with personal growth and the creation of a Growth TRAC? Reflecting on over 200 separate research studies, Dr. Gordon Lawrence, nationally known educator, author, and consultant, has described the *learning preferences* of the 16 different MBTI personality types. *Understanding your personality type will help you craft a Growth TRAC that is best suited to your learning preference.* Doing so will increase your engagement in the Growth TRACing process and your commitment to lifelong learning. How an ENTJ learns will look quite different from how an ISFP learns. *Therefore, your personality type should shape your Growth TRAC.* Failure to create a Growth TRAC that is sensitive to your personality will only create frustration and will likely lead to limited personal development.

Below I've summarized the learning preferences observed by Dr. Gordon Lawrence[76] for each of the personality types. I've

also included insights on how I believe these learning preferences impact the creation of a Growth TRAC.

1.   **Extraversion (E)** – The Extraversion type prefers growing with others. Their learning style leans on their network of relationships with whom they enjoy processing
ideas and thoughts aloud. Because Extraversion types
are very active and often stimulated by their environment, they typically enjoy growth steps that require
physical movement. One Extraversion type told me that
relationships not only help him grow, but they actually
help him *define* his growth areas. An Extraversion type's
Growth TRAC should consider the following:

- Training that is hands-on, active, and experiential.
  Extraversion types learn best by doing. They often
  embrace trial and error and readily plunge into something new.
- Group projects and learning in small groups where
  the opportunity exists for extensive interaction and
  dialogue.
- Resources coupled with the opportunity to discuss,
  teach, or debrief. If an Extraversion type reads a
  book, they may prefer doing so with a small group
  where they can discuss, and in some cases even
  teach, what they've learned. They don't like to keep
  what they learn to themselves.
- Interviews, surveys, and brainstorming sessions.
- Coaching from people who model ideas and values
  appealing to the Extraversion type.

- Shorter growth cycles (perhaps a three month Growth TRAC rather than twelve months) to allow for greater flexibility.
- Relationships and experiences will be especially important to the Extraversion type's Growth TRAC.

2.   **Introversion (I) –** Extraversion types enjoy public dialogue, but Introversion types prefer internal dialogue where they can privately process thoughts and ideas. "While Extraverts enjoy editing their ideas as they talk them out, Introverts want to edit privately."[77] An Introversion type's Growth TRAC should consider the following:

- Opportunities to listen to lectures, teachings, and discussions.
- Resources such as podcasts, CDs, books, and articles that stimulate thinking without the requirement to engage in dialogue. Reading can often be the preferred study style for an Introvert.
- One-on-one coaching, mentoring, and accountability relationships that the Introversion type chooses with appropriate time to prepare for meetings.
- Writing or journaling—this can help bring clarity to thoughts.
- Appropriate time for personal reflection.
- Opportunities to *observe* ideas, strategies, or methods in action without the pressure to turn outward.

3.   **Sensing (S)** – The Sensing types enjoy starting with
the familiar facts—understanding exactly where they are
right now—and then growing toward their desired destination. For the Sensing type, they prefer a clear, specific, step-by-step process for getting from where they are
to where they want to be. Their learning is factual and
concrete rather than intuitive. Furthermore, they want to
ensure their Growth TRAC is solid and void of any gaps.
A Sensing type's Growth TRAC should consider the following:

- Incorporating appropriate assessments to gauge
personal strengths and weaknesses. This will increase awareness of personal growth gaps and bring
clarity to appropriate growth steps.
- A diversity of growth steps that engage as many of
the senses as possible.
- A detailed and efficient plan that removes any doubt
of what it takes to reach specific growth targets.
Sensing types do not want to waste time learning
skills or facts that appear irrelevant. There must be a
meaningful and useful reason for every growth step.
- Training that is extremely practical, not theoretical.
- Learning that requires the observation and memorization of concrete details.
- Teaching that is presented in a specific and sequen-
tial manner without moving too quickly or touching
solely on the "high points."
- Resources and relationships that are unquestion-
ably relevant to the growth target and engage multiple senses. For example, reading only engages the

sense of sight, and therefore may be less appealing to the Sensing type unless it offers extremely practical information that can be immediately applied. For Sensing types, books may support the lesson rather than serve as the center of the lesson.

- Activities that provide immediate, hands-on experience.

4. **Intuition (N)** – Intuitive types are very concerned about the "why" not just the "what." They are not interested in learning something without first understanding the big picture. "They resist step-by-step instruction that doesn't start with the global concept first."[78] The Intuition type does not follow a clear, step-by-step process. Rather, they prefer a more intuitive approach to learning that avoids needless steps. "They like beginning new things more than continuing familiar things, but when their inspiration is sustained, it carries them through to finish what they start."[79] An Intuition type's Growth TRAC should consider the following:

- Clarity about the growth target (or goal) is essential. Intuition types must understand why they are growing in a particular area and must be inspired by a worthy goal. If you are an Intuition type, you may need to spend more time clarifying the growth goal (target) than developing the growth steps (roadmap).
- The Growth TRAC may need to be developed in stages. Because Intuition types prefer to be led by their intuition, their Growth TRAC needs enough structure to get them started but enough flexibility

to keep them engaged. Therefore, it may be wise to create a Growth TRAC in stages with no more than two growth steps in each stage. Once a step is completed in the roadmap portion of your Growth TRAC, you can determine your next growth step based on your intuitive gut feelings.

- Include enough new and fresh material—training, resources, relationships, and experiences—in your Growth TRAC to keep you fully engaged and energized. Intuition types need continual exposure to new concepts, ideas, and possibilities. This may require you to venture outside of your typical growth strategies and embrace more creative or challenging opportunities for learning.
- Identify and pursue regular accountability to ensure the Growth TRAC is kept in focus—especially if it is being developed in stages. This is particularly important if you're going to maintain alignment between your growth goal (target) and your growth steps (roadmap).
- Include assignments that require personal initiative and allow flexibility in how the assignments are executed.
- Include assignments that allow for creative expression and the opportunity to be inventive and original.
- Adopt a learning speed that assumes a brisk pace.

5.   **Thinking (T) –** The Thinking type values bringing order out of chaos or confusion. They tend to be problem-solvers, analyze data, and find flaws that need to be fixed. Thinking types learn best when they can concentrate on

their work without being distracted by emotional issues. A Thinking type's Growth TRAC should consider the following:

- A shift from goal-setting to problem-solving. Instead of creating personal growth targets (or goals), the Thinking type might consider creating personal growth problems to be solved. This may sound like nothing more than a difference in terminology, but understanding the goal as a problem to be solved might actually serve as a greater motivator for some Thinking types.
- Training and coaching presented in a logical manner with the opportunity to analyze problems and critique strategies, methods, or data.
- Case studies, field trips, and experiences that provide opportunity to learn by analyzing and critiquing.
- Challenges that require mastery of material.
- Resources such as books, articles, and case studies that present solutions to problems you might currently face. Any resource that presents a cause and effect relationship on a subject of interest will appeal to a Thinking type.
- Accountability and coaching relationships that encompass opportunities to question and challenge ideas.
- Growth opportunities free from emotional distractions.

6.   Feeling (F) – The Feeling type enjoys harmony and personal relationships. Therefore, relationships play an important role in learning and personal growth. A Feeling type's Growth TRAC should consider the following:

- Craft a Growth TRAC that will not only benefit you, but the people around you as well. In other words, choose growth targets and growth steps that will enrich relationships.
- Choose growth targets that are connected to the priorities, causes, core values, or relationships you care about deeply.
- Participate in training and classes with teachers who have relationships and personal rapport with students.
- Because of a value for interaction, relationships will prove especially meaningful.
- Gather or organize a group of friends who desire to grow in a similar area as you. Make the growth goal a small group focus.
- Include a trust-filled accountability relationship in your Growth TRAC.
- Read biographies that will help you learn valuable lessons from people you admire and respect. This will make what you learn more personal and relational.
- Include growth experiences, assignments, and activities that focus on serving or helping others.

7.   **Judging (J)** – The Judging type feels very energized by the idea of a Growth TRAC. They enjoy organization, clear plans, and predictable systems. Judging types excel with schedules and plans. A Judging type's Growth TRAC should consider the following:

- The Growth TRAC should be clearly organized and very exact. There should be no confusion about the expectations in the Judging type's Growth TRAC.
- Training should be well organized and systematically scheduled, and offer clear, executable plans. Training should have a clear and valuable point.
- Pursue schooling, certifications, or training that offer a degree, certificate, or reward upon completion. Judging types have a high value for getting things done and finishing what they start. They often prefer formal instruction.
- Embrace accountability relationships with clearly communicated standards for which you will be held accountable.
- Include growth activities and assignments that have a serious nature. You will tend to be suspicious of growth opportunities that appear too shallow and light-hearted.
- Carefully schedule every growth step into your calendar.
- Include deadlines for each growth step.
- Include celebrations in the Growth TRAC for achieving growth goals.

8.   **Perceiving (P)** – Perceiving types do not necessarily like preplanning because it can serve as a barrier to
gaining insight and information from their senses or
intuition. They have a high value for flexibility and the
greatest personal growth often comes in bursts or surg-
es. A Perceiving type's Growth TRAC should consider
the following:

- The aspect of Growth TRACing that can appeal to
  Perceiving types is the ability to *choose* a path for
  growth. In other words, Perceiving types should take
  advantage of the *customization* of their Growth TRAC.
  The sky is the limit and therefore the plan should be
  as unique as a fingerprint. Avoid routine sameness.
- Like the Intuition types, Perceiving types should consider creating a Growth TRAC in stages. This will
  keep the growth planning process fresh, flexible, and
  open to the spontaneity of a Perceiving type's growth
  preferences. Begin with a couple of growth steps
  and then revisit the Growth TRAC regularly to add
  appropriate next steps.
- Consider short-term growth goals. Because Perceiving types enjoy shifting attention from one thing to
  the next, growth goals that can be completed in a
  relatively short period of time will have greater appeal than goals that stretch over an entire year. This
  will help the Perceiving type deal with the tension
  between a plan and spontaneity. You might even allow "the moment" to define the Growth TRAC rather
  than the Growth TRAC to define the moments. This

will obviously require some balance to ensure you are staying on track.

- Engage in training that is new, on the edge, and presented in an out of the box format.
- Include reading in your Growth TRAC, but don't feel guilty for not finishing the book.
- Pursue one-time coaching appointments or interviews that will give you the information you need without having to commit to a series of appointments. This will add spontaneity to the value of coaching.
- Embrace accountability to ensure your personal growth gains traction. The flexibility of your Growth TRAC will need appropriate accountability to keep you moving forward.
- Include a variety of activities, assignments, and experiences that are creative, innovative, and engaging. Engagement will increase if growth assignments and activities feel like play yet genuinely contribute to personal growth. Pursuing growth goals that are connected with personal passions will help.
- Utilize the latest technology to execute your roadmap. This can help learning feel like play.

Your personality will (and should) shape your Growth TRAC. The learning preferences described above offer specific ideas to help you craft a plan that will lead to greater success in personal transformation. As you create your Growth TRAC, think about how your personality influences the answers to the four growth questions:

- What are my growth goals?
- How do I plan to grow?
- Who will hold me accountable for my growth?
- When and how will I evaluate my growth progress?

Four Ways Your Personality Shapes
Your Growth TRAC

To help you merge your personality type with your Growth TRAC, use the following four-question grid. These filtering questions will help you use your personality to further shape your Growth TRAC while keeping your learning preferences in check.

1.   **GOALS**: *How Does Your Personality Influence the Selection of Growth Goals (or Targets)?* Personality and goal selection are deeply intertwined. For example, a Sensing type enjoys concrete facts and a clear understanding of where they are right now. This helps them understand the size of the gap between where they are and where they want to be. To accurately define this gap, personal assessments are helpful. An assessment will help the Sensing type determine their strengths and weaknesses in a given growth area. This will enable them to understand current reality, and then select an appropriate growth goal based on that understanding. Intuition types, on the other hand, need to understand the "why" behind the "what." If they are going to grow, they have to see the 30,000-foot big picture purpose behind the growth. For the Intuition type, they need to spend *more*

time on the front end choosing and articulating the *right* growth target.

2. **CYCLE**: *How Should Your Personality Shape the Length of Your Growth Cycle?* A growth cycle refers to the length of your Growth TRAC. For example, you might have four growth targets that stretch over a 12-month growth cycle. Each goal may be a different length, but the overall cycle is one year. I believe personality should define the length of your growth cycle. A Judging type's Growth TRAC needs to be very predictable. Therefore, a longer growth cycle may work very well. However, a Perceiving type needs flexibility. They resist routine and prefer spontaneity. A shorter growth cycle may work better for the Perceiving type.

3. **ENERGY**: *What Energizes Your Personality?* Whatever energizes your personality should also energize your Growth TRAC. Dr. Debra Nelson and Dr. James Campbell Quick observe:

    > Introverts need quiet time to study, concentrate, and reflect on what they are learning. They think best when they are alone. Extraverts need to interact with other people, learning through the process of expressing and exchanging ideas with others. They think best in groups and while they are talking.[80]

    Time with people will energize the Extraversion type and time alone will energize the Introversion type. Their Growth TRACs should reflect this preference.

4.   **STEPS**: *Which Growth Steps Fit Naturally with Your Personality?* The four growth steps to include in a Growth TRAC include training, resources, relationships, and experiences. If you'll recall from chapter four, these four ingredients make up the "R" (Roadmap) part of your Growth TRAC. Understanding your personality will help you determine how these growth steps should be reflected in your Growth TRAC. For example, the Thinking type enjoys solving problems. The steps in his Growth TRAC—whether reading a book, gaining coaching, or engaging in an activity—need to provide the opportunity to analyze and critique. The Feeler type is very much about relationships. If she's going to read a book, there should be opportunity to discuss it with friends. She will no doubt find increased value in the relationship aspect of Growth TRACing. If she's going to attend a conference, she probably shouldn't go alone.

Let me conclude with one challenge. Don't allow your personality to become an excuse. For example, if you need to grow in your relationship with your spouse or your kids, but your personality type is more Introversion than Extraversion, this is not an excuse for relational dysfunction. And if you need to grow in the details of your budgeting skills, you cannot use the excuse that your personality hates structure and details. *Do your best to lean on the strengths of your personality to address the liabilities in your life.* Your personality should add life to your growth, not sap the life out of it. And when you create a Growth TRAC that is sensitive to your unique, God-given personality, you'll go much further and find greater fulfillment in your growth journey.

Sample Growth TRAC & Template

O n the following pages are samples of several Growth TRACs. Each Growth TRAC provides an example of what a personal growth plan might look like in various areas of your life. These are meant to be examples only. These samples will help you better understand how to craft a Growth TRAC that's specific and measurable.

In addition to the samples, you'll find blank templates that you can use to create your own Growth TRAC. As noted in chapter 4, please refer to Appendix A and Appendix B before creating your TRAC. Appendix A offers helpful assessment ideas and Appendix B provides valuable information on how your personality should shape your Growth TRAC.

Finally, if you feel overwhelmed, simply step back and narrow your focus. You might consider doing just one Growth TRAC to help you get started. Keep it simple. Don't put too much in the Growth TRAC. And don't let the examples below intimidate you. It's better to have one or two TRACs that are clear, specific, and measurable than to have so many growth goals that you defeat yourself before you start. Remember, your Growth TRAC has to work for YOU.

Growth Question		Growth TRAC
T	**TARGET** What is my growth goal?	SPIRITUAL: Deepen my understanding and personal application of the teachings of Jesus in the Sermon on the Mount.
R	**ROADMAP** How do I plan to grow? What Training, Resources, Relationships, & Experiences will I use as growth steps?	• Read the Sermon on the Mount in two versions (NIV and NLT). • Download a sermon series on the Sermon on the Mount. • Facilitate a 6-week small group on the Sermon on the Mount. • Identify the three portions of the Sermon on the Mount that are most deeply challenging to me at this season in my life and do an in-depth Bible study on those three passages. • Pinpoint a specific personal application point for each of the three passages, draft an accountability question for each, and share these with my accountability partner.
A	**ACCOUNTABILITY** Who will hold me accountable for my growth?	• Accountability Partner: Jason Smith • Accountability Questions: What progress are you making with your Sermon on the Mount reading and listening goals? When will you start your small group? What three points have you identified? How can I hold you accountable for those three points?
C	**CHECK-UP** When and how will I evaluate my growth progress?	Evaluate progress as follows: • Read the Sermon on the Mount by January 31. • Complete the Sermon on the Mount podcast by February 28. • Launch a Sermon on the Mount small group in March. • Pinpoint three major takeaways by April 10 and provide accountability questions to Jason for monthly accountability for the next six months.

	Growth Question	Growth TRAC
T	**TARGET** What is my growth goal?	SPIRITUAL: Cultivate a closer walk with God through consistent and meaningful prayer, Bible study, and Scripture memorization.
R	**ROADMAP** How do I plan to grow? What Training, Resources, Relationships, & Experiences will I use as growth steps?	• Schedule a personal prayer and devotional time from 6:30 – 7:00 am, Monday – Friday. • Interview my pastor on the topic of prayer. • Draft a list of 22 Scriptures (two per month beginning in February) that address the topics of wisdom, love, self-control, and leadership. • Create a waterproof version of my Scripture memory list and hang it in my shower. Review Scripture verses each morning to assist in the memory of two verses per month. • Do a character study of one Biblical leader— Moses. • Read the entire New Testament this year.
A	**ACCOUNTABILITY** Who will hold me accountable for my growth?	• First Monday of each week accountability meeting with James Davidson at 7:30 am at the local coffee shop. • Accountability Questions: How consistent has your prayer and Bible reading been this week? Quote the verses you've memorized this month. What are you learning from your character study on Moses? How far are you in the New Testament? How can I pray for you?
C	**CHECK-UP** When and how will I evaluate my growth progress?	Evaluate progress as follows: • Begin a morning prayer routine in January. • Create Scripture memorization list in February. • Interview pastor on prayer in May. • Begin study of Moses in September and complete by December.

	Growth Question	Growth TRAC
T	**TARGET** What is my growth goal?	MENTAL: Improve my skills in building and developing teams and address team dysfunction among our team.
R	**ROADMAP** How do I plan to grow? What Training, Resources, Relationships, & Experiences will I use as growth steps?	• Hire a leadership coach to help me create an effective hiring process and help me navigate conflict on the management team. • Purchase Patrick Lencioni's complete kit, The Five Dysfunctions of a Team, including book, field guide, video, facilitator's guide, participant workbooks, and assessments. • Have the entire team complete the Five Dysfunctions online assessment. • Read The Five Dysfunctions of a Team & field guide. • Schedule a team retreat using Patrick Lencioni's video and facilitator materials. • Identify & implement new ideas from the retreat for improved team relationships/performance. • Conduct monthly follow-up the first Wednesday of each month to continue team discussions.
A	**ACCOUNTABILITY** Who will hold me accountable for my growth?	• Monthly accountability with Jessica Cole • Accountability Questions: Who have you hired to serve as a team coach and when will they start? Have you ordered The Five Dysfunctions of a Team Kit? When and where is your team retreat? What have you learned from reading The Five Dysfunctions of a Team book and field guide? What happened in last month's team meeting and how are you implementing new plans?
C	**CHECK-UP** When and how will I evaluate my growth progress?	Evaluate progress as follows: • Hire coach in January. • Order Kit in February. • Have assessments and book reading completed in March. • Complete field guide in April. • Schedule Retreat for April. • Begin monthly team meetings in May.

	Growth Question	Growth TRAC
T	**TARGET** What is my growth goal?	FINANCIAL: Create and implement a personal financial plan that will establish $5,000 in an emergency fund, eliminate $10,000 in debt, and set up a college fund for my kids.
R	**ROADMAP** How do I plan to grow? What Training, Resources, Relationships, & Experiences will I use as growth steps?	• Sign up for and complete Dave Ramsey's course, Financial Peace University. • Create and implement a zero-based budget with the maximum amount possible allocated toward early debt retirement. • Hold a garage sale, sell old books on Amazon.com, and sell the motorcycle to earn money for the emergency fund. • Close my credit card accounts. • Allocate all additional non-regular income (bonuses, tax refund, and additional unexpected income) toward debt retirement. • Meet with a financial advisor to set up a college fund for the kids.
A	**ACCOUNTABILITY** Who will hold me accountable for my growth?	• Monthly accountability with Greg Logan • Accountability Questions: Are you living according to your zero-based budget? What challenges are you facing? What needs to be adjusted? When is your garage sale? Have you sold your old books and motorcycle? How much debt did you pay off this month? What's your savings up to? Did you close all credit card accounts? What did your financial advisor say about college funding?
C	**CHECK-UP** When and how will I evaluate my growth progress?	Evaluate progress: • Sign up for FPU course beginning in February. • Create zero-based budget in February. • Sell motorcycle and books in February. • Conduct garage sale in May. • Meet with Financial Advisor about college funding in September.

		Growth Question	Growth TRAC
T		**TARGET** What is my growth goal?	RELATIONAL: Invest time cultivating deeper relational health with my family.
R		**ROADMAP** How do I plan to grow? What Training, Resources, Relationships, & Experiences will I use as growth steps?	• Be home from work by 5:30 pm Monday – Friday • Leave my computer at the office a minimum of three days per week. • Take the kids to school two mornings per week (Tuesdays & Thursdays). • Put the kids to bed three nights per week with a story time. • Subscribe to "CUE Box" from the ReThink Group as a tool to connect with my kids and deepen conversations on values and character. • Download the "Parent CUE App" on my phone as a tool to help me connect with my kids around important virtues. • Schedule and plan two date nights per month with my wife. • Schedule a one-week family vacation in June. • Schedule and a weekend getaway with my wife in September. • Sign-up and participate in the marriage small group at the church.
A		**ACCOUNTABILITY** Who will hold me accountable for my growth?	• Monthly accountability with Eric Johnson on the third Thursday morning of the month at 7:30 AM • Accountability Questions: How often did you arrive home on time this month? Describe the quality of your story time with your kids this month? What has been the biggest impact of the "CUE Box" and the Parent CUE app with your kids this month? Have you been helping your wife by taking the kids to school twice per week? Where are you going on vacation and how's the plan coming? What are you learning and applying from the marriage small group at church?
C		**CHECK-UP** When and how will I evaluate my growth progress?	Evaluate progress as follows with my accountability partner: • In January begin taking the kids to school • In the month of February, schedule and plan our June vacation, subscribe to "CUE Box," and begin using the CUE app. • In the month of June, schedule and plan our September getaway • Sign up for a marriage small group to begin in September

	Growth Question	Growth TRAC
T	**TARGET** What is my growth goal?	PHYSICAL: Develop healthy eating and exercise habits and lose 20 pounds.
R	**ROADMAP** How do I plan to grow? What Training, Resources, Relationships, & Experiences will I use as growth steps?	• Join the new gym that opened near my home. • Workout four times per week for one hour— Monday, Tuesday, & Thursday afternoons from 5:00 – 6:00 pm, and Saturday mornings from 8:30 –9:30 am with David Baxter. • Completely cut soft drinks from my diet. • Secure a trainer for the first three months. • Get a physical.
A	**ACCOUNTABILITY** Who will hold me accountable for my growth?	• Weekly accountability with David Baxter. • Accountability Questions: Have you cut soft drinks from your diet? What is your weight this week? Have you scheduled a physical? (Because David is my workout partner, he will know how often I exercise.)
C	**CHECK-UP** When and how will I evaluate my growth progress?	Evaluate progress as follows: • Get a physical and cut soft drinks in January. • Join the new gym and begin exercising in February. • Lose two pounds per month for 10 months (beginning in February).

	Growth Question	Growth TRAC
T	**TARGET** What is mygrowth goal?	
R	**ROADMAP** How do I plan to grow? What Training, Resources, Relationships, & Experiences will I use as growth steps?	• • • •
A	**ACCOUNTABILITY** Who will hold me accountable for my growth?	• Accountability Partner: • Accountability Frequency: • Accountability Questions:
C	**CHECK-UP** When and how will I evaluate my growth progress?	Evaluate progress as follows: • • •

	Growth Question	Growth TRAC
T	**TARGET** What is mygrowth goal?	
R	**ROADMAP** How do I plan to grow? What Training, Resources, Relationships, & Experiences will I use as growth steps?	• • • •
A	**ACCOUNTABILITY** Who will hold me accountable for my growth?	• Accountability Partner: • Accountability Frequency: • Accountability Questions:
C	**CHECK-UP** When and how will I evaluate my growth progress?	Evaluate progress as follows: • • •

	Growth Question	Growth TRAC
T	**TARGET** What is mygrowth goal?	
R	**ROADMAP** How do I plan to grow? What Training, Resources, Relationships, & Experiences will I use as growth steps?	• • • •
A	**ACCOUNTABILITY** Who will hold me accountable for my growth?	• Accountability Partner: • Accountability Frequency: • Accountability Questions:
C	**CHECK-UP** When and how will I evaluate my growth progress?	Evaluate progress as follows: • • •

	Growth Question	Growth TRAC
T	**TARGET** What is mygrowth goal?	
R	**ROADMAP** How do I plan to grow? What Training, Resources, Relationships, & Experiences will I use as growth steps?	• • • •
A	**ACCOUNTABILITY** Who will hold me accountable for my growth?	• Accountability Partner: • Accountability Frequency: • Accountability Questions:
C	**CHECK-UP** When and how will I evaluate my growth progress?	Evaluate progress as follows: • • •

Notes

Chapter 1

[1] Steve Moore, *The Dream Cycle: Leveraging the Power of Personal Growth* (Indianapolis, IN: Wesleyan Publishing House, 2004), 32.

[2] Craig Groeschel, *Creating Personal Spiritual Momentum*, Catalyst One Day, p. 24, May 18, 2009, Dallas, Texas.

Chapter 2

[3] Matthew 5:3 (NIV)

[4] Bruce Winston, *Be a Leader for God's Sake* (Virginia Beach, VA: Regent University, 2002), 22.

[5] Matthew 25:31-46 (NIV)

[6] "Lisa Beamer's Strength," NBC News, Retrieved February 12, 2009, from http://www.msnbc.msn.com/id/3080111/page/2/

[7] Romans 8:28 (NIV)

Chapter 3

[8] Colossians 1:1 (The Message)

[9] 2 Timothy 4:7 (NIV)

[10] 2 Timothy 4:13 (The Message)

[11] "Nearly One in Two Americans Read a Book Last Year According to Bowker's 2008 PubTrack Consumer Survey," May 29, 2009, Retrieved January 2, 2012, from http://www.bowker.com/index.php/press-releases/564

Chapter 4

[12] "Interesting New Year's Resolution Statistics," December 11, 2008, Retrieved January 2, 2012, from http://www.steveshapiro.com/2008/12/11/interesting-new-years-resolution-statistics/

[13] Reggie McNeal, *Missional Renaissance: Changing the Scorecard for the Church* (San Francisco: Jossey-Bass, 2009), 92.

[14] I was introduced to a detailed concept of growth planning by Steve Moore who articulates the four ingredients to a plan in his book, *The Dream Cycle, Leveraging the Power of Personal Growth.* For simplicity, I have presented these concepts as a Growth TRAC accompanied by four foundational growth questions.

15 Marcus Buckingham and Donald O. Clifton, *The Strengths Revolution*, Retrieved September 3, 2007, from http://gmj.gallup.com/content/547/The-Strengths-Revolution.aspx

16 Maximum Impact Podcast, June 13, 2007, http://www.maximumimpact.com/podcast/faq.aspx retrieved September 3, 2007

17 Joseph Carroll, "Workers' Average Commute Round Trip is 46 Minutes in a Typical Day," August 24, 2007, Retrieved April 26, 2012, from http://www.gallup.com/poll/28504/workers-average-commute-roundtrip-minutes-typical-day.aspx

18 Mark Batterson, *In a Pit with a Lion on a Snowy Day* (Colorado Springs, CO: Multnomah Books, 2006), 44.

Chapter 5

19 "Fascinating facts about the invention of Play-Doh," Retrieved September 5, 2009, from http://www.ideafinder.com/history/inventions/playdoh.htm

20 About Play-Doh, Retrieved September 5, 2009, from Hasbro's website at http://www.hasbro.com/playdoh/en_US/About.cfm

21 Matthew 15:6 (NIV)

22 Proverbs 13:14 (The Message)

[23] Charles Colson and Harold Fickett, *The Faith: Given Once, For All* (Grand Rapids, MI: Zondervan, 2008), 53.

[24] Colson and Fickett, p. 51

[25] English Bible History, retrieved December 29, 2008, from http://www.greatsite.com/timeline-english-bible-history/

[26] Erwin McManus, *An Unstoppable Force: Daring to Become the Church God Had in Mind* (Loveland, CO: Group Publishing, 2001), 188.

Chapter 6

[27] William Wilberforce: Antislavery Politician, retrieved September 29, 2009, from http://www.christianitytoday.com/ch/131christians/activists/wilberforce.html?start=1

[28] William Wilberforce: Antislavery Politician, retrieved September 29, 2009, from http://www.christianitytoday.com/ch/131christians/activists/wilberforce.html

[29] Why Name the School After William Wilberforce?, retrieved September 29, 2009, from http://www.wilberforceschool.org/38436.ihtml

[30] William Wilberforce: Antislavery Politician, retrieved September 29, 2009, from http://www.christianitytoday.com/ch/131christians/activists/wilberforce.html

[31] Americans Watch More TV Than Ever; Web and Mobile Video Up Too, Retrieved March 5, 2010, from http://blog.nielsen.com/nielsenwire/online_mobile/americans-watching-more-tv-than-ever/#more-11915

[32] Reprinted with permission of the publisher, From *The Laws of Lifetime Growth*, p. 95 copyright© 2006 by Dan Sullivan & Catherine Nomura, Berrett-Koehler Publishers, Inc., San Francisco, CA. All rights reserved. www.bkconnection.com.

[33] William Wilberforce: Antislavery Politician, retrieved September 29, 2009, from http://www.christianitytoday.com/ch/131christians/activists/wilberforce.html?start=1

[34] Romans 12:2 (The Message)

[35] Proverbs 15:22 (NIV)

[36] Andy Stanley, *The Next Generation Leader* (Sisters, OR: Multnomah Publishers, Inc., 2003), 106.

Chapter 7

[37] Wright Brothers Biography, Retrieved October 9, 2009, from http://www.notablebiographies.com/We-Z/Wright-Brothers.html

[38] The Wright Brothers: Wilbur and Orville Wright, Retrieved October 9, 2009, from http://www.wright-house.com/wright-brothers/Wrights.html

[39] Mark Eppler, *The Wright Way* (New York, NY: Amacom, 2004), 119.

[40] Eppler, p. 127.

[41] James 2:17 (NIV)

[42] Dr. William R. Yount, *Created to Learn* (Nashville, TN: Broadman & Holman Publishers, 1996), 9.

[43] Ephesians 4:23-24 (The Message)

[44] Craig Groeschel, *The Christian Atheist: Believing in God but Living as if He Doesn't Exist* (Grand Rapids, MI: Zondervan, 2010).

Chapter 8

[45] Quoted in Richard Farson and Ralph Keyes, *Whoever Makes the Most Mistakes Wins: The Paradox of Innovation* (New York: Free Press, 2002), 32.

[46] Andy Stanley, *The Next Generation Leader* (Sisters, OR: Multnomah Publishers, Inc., 2003), 45.

[47] Leadership Through the Ages: A Collection of Favorite Quotations (New York: Miramax Books, 2003), 94.

Chapter 9

[48] Jared Fogle, retrieved January 7, 2012, from http://www.nndb. com/people/955/000044823/

[49] Jared S. Fogle, retrieved January 7, 2012, from http://www. pr.com/company-profile/employees-biography/1214-1061

[50] Luke 6:43-45 (The Message)

[51] Quoted in John C. Maxwell, Stephen R. Graves, & Thomas G. Addington, *Life@Work: Marketplace Success for People of Faith*, (Nashville, TN: Thomas Nelson, 2005), 8.

[52] 1 Corinthians 11:1 (NIV)

[53] Regi Campbell, *Mentor Like Jesus* (Nashville, TN: B & H Publishing Group, 2009), 12. Used by permission.

[54] Dr. Tim Elmore, *Nurturing the Leader Within Your Child*, (Nashville, TN: Thomas Nelson, 2001), 5.

[55] Matthew 12:33b (The Message)

Chapter 10

[56] The Inner City 100: True Grit, Retrieved May 14, 2010, from http://www.businessweek.com/smallbiz/content/jun2009/ sb2009061_065785.htm?chan=smallbiz_special+report+-

+inner+city+100+2009_special+report%3A+inner+ci
ty+100+2009

[57]   About Bill, Retrieved September 6, 2009, from http://www.
bill-strickland.org/aboutbill.html

[58]   Bill Strickland, *Make the Impossible Possible*, (New York, Doubleday, 2007), 3.

[59]   Strickland, p. 35.

[60]   Strickland, p. 28.

[61]   Strickland, p. 9.

[62]   Luke 12:48, (NIV).

[63]   Mentor Reader: Clinton Articles on Mentoring (written over
the years 1993-2005). Mentoring – An Informal Training Model,
Dr. Bobby Clinton, retrieved February 5, 2009 from http://www.
bobbyclinton.com/articles/downloads/MentoringReader.pdf
from p. 5.

[64]   Bill Strickland with Vince Rause, *Make the Impossible Possible*
(New York: Doubleday, 2007), 46-47.

[65]   *Leadership Through the Ages: A Collection of Favorite Quotations*
(New York: Miramax Books, 2003), 81.

[66]   Proverbs 27:17 (NIV)

Chapter 11

[67] Permission to use this blog post was retrieved on March 17, 2009.

[68] 1 Thessalonians 1:4-8 (NIV)

[69] Dr. Bruce H. Lipton (www.brucelipton.com), *The Biology of Belief*, (Santa Rosa, CA, Mountain of Love/Elite Books, 2005),145.

[70] Lipton, p. 146.

[71] Lipton, p. 147.

[72] Dr. Shirley Peddy, *The Art of Mentoring: Lead, Follow and Get Out of the Way,* (Houston, TX, Bullion Books, 2001), 24-25.

Chapter 12

[73] Bill Strickland, *Make the Impossible Possible* (New York, Doubleday, 2007), 21.

[74] Strickland, p. 20-21.

[75] Reggie McNeal, *Missional Renaissance: Changing the Scorecard for the Church* (San Francisco, CA: Jossey-Bass, 2009), 9.

Appendix B

[76] Dr. Gordon Lawrence, *Looking at Type® and Learning Styles: Using Psychological Type to Make Learning Personally Effective* (Gainesville, FL: Center for Applications of Psychological Type, Inc.).

[77] Dr. Gordon Lawrence, p. 14.

[78] Dr. Gordon Lawrence, p. 15.

[79] Dr. Gordon Lawrence, p. 15.

[80] Debra L. Nelson & James Campbell Quick, *Organizational Behavior: Foundations, Realities, & Challenges* 5th *ed.* (Mason, OH: South-Western, 2006), 185.

——— Acknowledgements ———

The message of this book has been inside of me for many years. While many people have encouraged me in my own growth journey, and in the development of this book, I'd like to say a special thanks to the following people:

- *Jesus.* Thank you for your unwaivering love, grace, and compassion. You imprinted the message of this book on my heart, and you are ever patient with me as I seek to grow. May you be glorified through this work.

- *Karen.* Thank you for that first conversation where you encouraged me to write this book. Your belief in me and your faithful love are a constant source of joy. Your growth inspires me to keep growing. I love you always!

- *Ashley.* Many times while writing this book I reflected on how lucky I am to have you as my daughter. I am so proud of you and so glad I get to walk alongside of you in your own growth journey. I love you!

- *Dad and Mom.* Thank you for your constant prayers, encouragement, and support. This long writing journey has come to a close and I'm so glad you cheered me on all along the way. I love you!

- Roy & Pearla. Thank you for your continual words of affirmation as this project moved to completion. Your love and support is appreciated more than you know.

- *Bill & Nancy Clark.* Thank you for encouraging, praying for, and investing in our dreams. Your unbelievable gift of hospitality has blessed our family more times than we can count.

- *Jeff Galley.* Thanks for being a friend who always believed in the message of this book. You continually sharpen my thinking, challenge my growth, and help me gain perspective.

- *Derek & Jennifer Moffatt.* Thank you for your friendship and your sincere belief in me and Karen. Your constant affirmation inspires us to take new risks that are bound to make us grow. It's great to take the journey with faithful friends.

- *Steve Moore.* Thanks for your coaching in personal growth and life purpose. You helped me understand who God made me to be and your passion for personal growth is contagious.

- *Darius & Cindy Johnston.* Thanks for modeling what it means to follow Christ, and for making repeated investments in my personal growth over many years.

- *Brannon Golden.* Thank you for your masterful work with words. You have been more than an editor to me...you've been a mentor.

- *Trisha Heddlesten.* Thank you for helping me complete the editing journey. Your insight and perspective helped me finish well.

About the Author

STEPHEN BLANDINO is the Lead Pastor of 7 City Church, an author, blogger, and leadership coach. With over 20 years of experience in nonprofit leadership, Stephen is passionate about helping people engage in personal growth, develop their full leadership capacity, and produce effective, Kingdom-advancing ministry. He holds a Master's in Organizational Leadership and has trained thousands of leaders across the United States. Stephen lives in the Fort Worth, Texas area with his wife Karen and their daughter Ashley.

Contact Stephen Blandino

Stephen Blandino blogs regularly at stephenblandino.com and is available to speak on personal growth and leadership topics for keynote, half-day, and full day events. He also provides coaching opportunities and consulting. To learn more or to contact Stephen, connect with him at:

- Blog: stephenblandino.com
- Twitter: twitter.com/stephenblandino
- Facebook: facebook.com/stephen.blandino

Ready to Grow Yourself and the People You Influence?

Stephen Blandino

Stephen Blandino can help you and your team maximize and leverage personal growth to produce powerful results personally and organizationally. Whether you work with a business, nonprofit, local church, or organization, Stephen will help you:

- Close your personal growth gaps
- Develop a customized personal growth TRAC
- Experience the power of the five levels of personal growth
- Intentionally invest in others' growth
- Develop an organizational growth culture

If you want to take the lid off your growth, or your team's growth, contact Stephen today to learn more about his speaking, coaching, and consulting.

"Stephen Blandino is one of the greatest leadership trainers and developers of curriculum I have ever met. He is an incredible asset to the Kingdom of God at large."

SCOTT WILSON, Senior Pastor, The Oaks, Author of *Steering Through Chaos, The Next Level,* and *Act Normal*

"Stephen really gets the church. His content on church strategy is some of the best I've ever heard. You will not be disappointed in what he brings to the table for you and your team."

JUSTIN LATHROP, Director of Strategic Relations, General Council of the Assemblies of God

Find Out More at www.StephenBlandino.com

Made in the USA
Charleston, SC
01 September 2012